AF251063

THE VATICAN ORACLE

BROCARD SEWELL

The Vatican Oracle

DUCKWORTH

First published in 1970 by
Gerald Duckworth & Company Limited
3 Henrietta Street, London W.C.2

SBN 7156 0518 6

*Printed in Great Britain
by Ebenezer Baylis & Son Limited
The Trinity Press, Worcester, and London*

To FRANCES HOROVITZ

CONTENTS

INTRODUCTION

On July 25th 1968 Pope Paul VI issued his encyclical letter "Humanae Vitae", On the Right Order of the Procreation of Children. In it the Pope reaffirmed the condemnation in 1930 by Pope Pius XI of all forms of birth control as morally evil, with only two exceptions: total abstention from the use of sex in marriage, or the use of the so-called "safe" or infertile period.

Within twenty-four hours of the encyclical's publication it was evident that the Roman Catholic Church was facing its severest crisis since the Reformation. Earlier in the present century the Modernist crisis had shaken the Church of Rome to its foundations; but the building had stood firm. The religious thinkers who were called "Modernists" were relatively few in number; their writings were read, for the most part, by philosophers and theologians only. In England Father George Tyrrell had a larger public for his books; but the works of Père Lagrange, Maurice Blondel, the abbé Loisy, Archbishop Mignot, Lucien Laberthonière, and Ernesto Bonauiti, were read mostly by specialists. The aim of all these writers, mistaken though some of them were in their methods, was to interpret Christianity in terms that would be understood by the men and women of a scientific age, for whom the old scholastic language of religious discourse was unconvincing or meaningless. This meant making the fullest apologetic use of modern developments in philosophy and in the historical and biblical sciences. There was never a Modernist "movement" in any formal sense. Apart from the general aims that these and other writers shared they had no common programme and were not organised in any formal association.

In the face of the challenge that these thinkers posed, the conservatives in the Vatican, believing, as conservatives so often do, that all new ways of thinking are corrosive and rebellious, reacted with great severity, and "Modernism" was stamped out.

If a less rigid and uncomprehending spirit had prevailed in the Vatican at the time the chaff would have been quietly separated from the wheat of the new thought, and the Catholic Church would not have found itself committed to fighting a series of rearguard actions which it could not hope to win, the latest of these being the battle over contraception.

Modernism was formally condemned by Pope Pius X in two fulminating documents, the decree "Lamentabili" and the encyclical "Pascendi dominici gregis", both issued in 1907. The encyclical listed a long series of alleged Modernist errors, and to support it a comprehensive Anti-Modernist Oath was drawn up. This had to be taken, until recently, by all clerics holding benefices, all seminary professors, candidates for holy orders, and bishops elect. The oath lingers on today in attenuated form.

These anti-Modernist measures were effective, and the Pope had little difficulty in calling his troops to order. But the cost of the conformity which had been so ruthlessly secured was high.

Some of the movement's ablest figures, such as the two laymen Maurice Blondel and Baron Friedrich von Hügel, managed uneasily to escape condemnation; others, among them Lagrange, the foremost Catholic biblical scholar of his day, remained under suspicion, and suffered various kinds of restriction and inhibition. Others were excommunicated. Some of these, among them Father Tyrrell, retired into private life; others left the Church. In one way or another most of the ablest thinkers of the day in the papal communion were either discouraged or extinguished.

The Modernists' ideas had little effect on the Catholic faithful. In England Father Tyrrell's gracefully written books were no doubt read, or at least glanced at, in the Catholic drawing-rooms of Mayfair and Kensington, but their greater circulation was among non-Catholics. Even among the Roman Catholic clergy the works of Modernist writers were not much studied, except by seminary professors whose business it was to warn their students off the ideas which these books contained. Most priests derived their knowledge of the new trends of thought from the "Syllabus", the encyclical "Pascendi", and the Anti-Modernist Oath.

In 1907, largely as a result of the First Vatican Council, of 1870, a high monarchic and near-absolutist idea of the Papacy was in the ascendant in the Catholic Church. This Council had reaffirmed the papal primacy in near-ultramontane terms, and had upgraded the traditional belief, which had not hitherto commanded universal assent among Catholics, in the Pope's "infallibility", to the status of a dogma, belief in which was necessary for salvation. In spite of the careful wording of the infallibility definition, one of its results was to give a new impetus to the tendency among Catholics to look on the Pope as a kind of oracle, or organ of revelation, which could produce infallibly correct answers to every question concerning the belief or conduct of Christians.

Since 1870 the popes themselves have encouraged this tendency, perhaps unwittingly, by their readiness to pour out encyclical letters to the bishops and faithful in communion with the Apostolic See at the slightest provocation. Most of these documents, all of them couched in high-sounding, and at times almost incomprehensible, curial language, are now museum pieces; though some, such as Leo XIII's "Rerum Novarum" (On the Condition of the Working Classes) and Pius XI's "Mitt brennender sorge" (on the errors of national socialism) are noble expressions of pastoral care.

As well as writing frequent encyclical letters, recent popes have spent a great deal of time in delivering addresses to the crowds of pilgrims which the facilities of modern transport bring in ever-increasing numbers to "The golden roof, the marble walls/The Vatican's majestic halls", as Cardinal Wiseman puts it in his baroque hymn, so dear to English Roman Catholics, "Full in the panting heart of Rome". With the aristocratic Pius XII the spate of papal oratory reached its zenith. Ever ready to address audiences of doctors, nurses, midwives, philosophers, lawyers, railwaymen, bee-keepers, noblemen, grocers, soldiers, sailors, airmen, and motorists, this pope always provided an appropriate and carefully prepared discourse for each group that he received.

All this, and many other factors besides, encouraged an un-critical "papolatry", which, fostered by the byzantine splendours of the pontifical court, was bound in time to produce a strong reaction. It came, explosively, when Pope Paul VI issued his encyclical letter "Humanae Vitae". This momentous document, affecting the majority of Catholics in the most intimate area of their personal lives, was issued by the Pope alone, just after the decrees of the Second Vatican Council had stressed the idea of collegiality[1] in church government. The encyclical was published after a long delay and much vacillation on the part of the Pope. During these years of uncertainty Catholics had been led to believe from the utterances of theologians, including bishops and cardinals and even the Pope himself, that some reassessment and modification of the Church's current teaching on the matter of birth control was possible, if not probable.

In an address given on July 23rd 1964 the Pope announced that "the Church" was studying the birth control question, and that "In the meantime we must say openly that up to now we have not sufficient reason to consider the rules laid down by Pius XII in this matter to be out of date and therefore not binding." This at least meant that the Pope believed it *possible* that the teaching could be revised.

In the same discourse the Pope had affirmed that the Church would have to "proclaim the law of God in the light of the scientific, social, and psychological truth which in these times have undergone new and very ample study and documentation".

At a session of the Second Vatican Council in October 1964 Cardinal Suenens, archbishop of Malines, said:

The Commission [established to advise the Pope on the birth control question] will have to examine whether the classical doctrine . . . takes sufficient account of the new insights in modern science. We have made some progress since Aristotle, and we have discovered the complexity of the reality where what is biological interferes with what is psychological and the conscious with the subconscious. New possibilities are constantly being discovered in man in his power to direct the course of nature. . . . Who does not see that thus we are perhaps being led to further inquiries on the question of what is according to nature or against nature? . . . I beg of you, my brothers; let us avoid a new Galileo case.

At the same session of the Council the Partriarch of Antioch, Maximos IV, said:

Frankly, ought not the official positions of the Church on this matter to be revised in the light of modern science, both theological and medical, psychological and sociological? . . . And moreover are we not in the right to ask ourselves if certain official positions are not to be attributed to out-dated conceptions and perhaps also to a psychosis of celibates who are strangers to this sector of life? Are we not, without wishing it, burdened by that Manichaean conception of man and of the world for which the work of the flesh, vitiated in itself, is only tolerated in view of the child?

Is the external biological correctness of actions the sole criterion of morality here, independently of the life of the couple, its moral climate as a marriage and as a family, and the weighty imperative of prudence, the fundamental rule of all our human activity? . . .

Far be it from me to minimise the delicacy and the gravity of the subject, as well as possible abuses; but here as elsewhere is it not the duty of the Church to educate the moral sense of her children, to train them to a moral, personal, and communal responsibility that is profoundly mature in Christ, rather than to envelop them in a network of prescriptions and commandments and to ask them purely and simply to conform to this with their eyes shut? Let us see things as they are and not as we would wish them to be. Otherwise we run the danger of talking in a wilderness. It is thus a question of the future of the Church's mission in the world.

In an article in *The Tablet* as late as May 8th 1968 the Cardinal Archbishop of Westminster, writing of the protracted delay in the publication of the Pope's promised decision on birth control, spoke of the "isolation" of the Pope from the bishops, and said that in the matter of birth control the ordinary teaching authority of the Church seemed to have lost its nerve. "If indeed," Dr Heenan bluntly said, "the old principles are to be adapted to the changed condition of our time, Catholics resent this long period of suspense." The Cardinal could scarcely have said more clearly that in his view a change or modification of the Church's stand on this matter was possible. In the same article he noted that "today in the same town, and even in the same parish, priests in the confessional offer conflicting advice."

It was an inevitable consequence of the delay over the papal pronouncement that many priests, as well as their people, came to feel that the former law was now at least doubtful, and therefore not of strict obligation. This view enabled many priests to show a more understanding and less inflexible attitude when they had to deal with this matter in the confessional.

A further, and equally inevitable, consequence of the delay was that although bishops might be unwilling to speak before the Pope had spoken, and theologians and other specialists might continue to spin their subtle arguments this way or that, large numbers of the laity began to feel that they must make up their own minds on the matter in accordance with their consciences.

When the Pope's decision did eventually come, it was received, except by ultra-conservative Catholics, with dismay and incredulity, as much because of the manner in which it was issued as because of its content. It was not surprising, therefore, that when on the following Sunday a paternalist pastoral letter from the Archbishop of Southwark was read in the churches and chapels of his diocese it should have met with some protest. At a church in Surrey some thirty people walked out after hearing priests who had done their best to help people to solve their problems in ways that would be at once Christian and human denounced as "false and devious advisers" who had misled "our poor simple people".

Many of these "simple people" must have asked themselves why the Holy Father, if he had known all along that the teaching could not be changed, had set up a commission of sixty members to advise him about it, and had taken four years to consider the matter before giving his verdict. They knew also, if they had read their *Universe*,[2] that all but four members of the Pope's commission of some sixty cardinals, bishops, priests, doctors, and fathers and mothers of families, had not only stated their belief that the teaching *could* be changed, but had positively recommended that it *should* be changed.

In some churches of the Southwark diocese priests reading the pastoral letter omitted this reference to their fellow-clergy, whose sincerity they respected, even if they might disagree with their views, and in one parish the incumbent, a canon of the chapter of St George's cathedral, practically rewrote the whole letter before reading it to his people.

The Archbishop read the letter himself to a very large open-air congregation of pilgrims assembled at the shrine of the Blessed Virgin at Aylesford in Kent. It was reported in *The Times* and *The Guardian* the next morning that after the letter had been read there was a spontaneous outburst of applause. The applause was not in fact spontaneous, but had been arranged and led by a small group of elderly feminine devotees.

Commenting on the encyclical soon after its publication the Archbishop of Durban, Dr Denis Hurley, took a very different line from that of his confrère at Southwark. Dr Hurley said that although he believed the Pope had the right to make the decision, it would be dishonest for him to say that he agreed either with the Pope's method of consultation or its result—sentiments for expressing which a number of priests in England had meanwhile been suspended from the exercise of their functions. Calling on national and regional episcopal conferences throughout the world to declare their attitude to the encyclical, Dr Hurley said: "As brothers of Pope Paul in the episcopate, bishops cannot shrink from the issue of how they think the authority of their senior brother should be exercised. To discuss it with him is not disloyalty, but speaking the truth in love."

This is exactly what happened. In spite of the insistence of Vatican spokesmen and of the Vatican newspaper *Osservatore Romano*, and of the Pope himself in his address to the bishops of Colombia on the occasion of his visit to Bogotà, that the encyclical on birth control must be accepted by all without qualification, an impressive series of bishops' conferences has affirmed, both for priests and people, the right of conscientious dissent.[3]

Some of these statements by the bishops are rather ambivalently phrased, and pay fulsome tribute to the Pope's good intentions and to the "noble" character of his pronouncement taken as a whole; but they make it clear that the primacy of conscience is not in dispute. The statement of the English and Welsh bishops took this line, seeming to give total submission to the papal teaching, yet allowing for the possibility of dissent. Considering the weight of ultra-conservative opinion on the episcopal bench, this was rather better than might have been expected; but the statement caused some offence by quoting from the encyclical a passage addressed to Catholic married couples which said that "if sin should still keep its hold over them, let them not be discouraged, but rather have recourse with humble perseverance to the mercy of God which is poured forth in the sacrament of Penance": i.e., in confession.

Since numbers of Catholics believed that there was nothing sinful in the practice of birth control as such, there was no reason why they should mention it in confession, and they resented being told to do so.

Some bishops' statements have explicitly upheld this position; notably that of the bishops of Scandinavia and Finland, which says that "if someone, from weighty and well-considered reasons, cannot become convinced by the arguments of the encyclical, it has always been conceded that he is allowed to have a different view from that presented in a non-infallible statement of the Church. No one should be considered a bad Catholic because he is of such a dissenting opinion."

Advising priests who may be consulted by married couples, the bishops of Scandinavia and Finland go on to say that if a married man or woman deviates out of conscientious conviction from the norm laid down by the encyclical "there may be no sin that must be confessed or that excludes the person from Holy Communion".

Nothing could be plainer than that, and it is in direct contradiction to the instructions of the bishops of England and Wales. The Austrian hierarchy, among others, has issued a statement to the same effect as that of the Scandinavian. Many other hierarchies have taken a similar line. But some, notably those of the United States, Scotland, and Ireland, have maintained the older, familiar Roman Catholic rigorism, and insist that the Pope's teaching must not be questioned.

How has it come about, and so suddenly, that the leader of the most authoritarian Church in the world now finds himself confronted with the rejection by a large part of his flock of his solemn teaching on a matter of Christian morality? That is what this book is about. It came to be written as a result of a letter from the author which was published in the correspondence columns of *The Times* on August 5th 1968, one of the first of many letters which that paper was to publish from Catholic priests and laity expressing their inability to accept the teaching of the encyclical.

At that time I was living in a religious house in the Roman Catholic diocese of Southwark, as I had been for most of the past fourteen years. Southwark priests were well represented among the general body of dissenters from the encyclical, and the reaction of the archbishop and his vicar-general was one of panic. The priests who had publicly expressed their dissent were at once suspended from preaching and hearing confessions, and the two who belonged to religious orders were transferred by their superiors to houses outside the diocese in the hope of avoiding further trouble. (One of them was lucky enough to be sent to pass the winter in Naples.) None of the suspended priests was formally charged with any "crime", or given the opportunity to defend himself before a properly constituted tribunal.

My letter to *The Times* read as follows:

Sir,

The publication of the encyclical letter "Humanae Vitae" shows, if nothing else, that the Orthodox and other Eastern Churches are fully justified in their mistrust of the papal office as it has developed over the centuries since the Great Schism. The "primacy of love" known to the early undivided Church has long since been replaced by the "Roman", and indeed Italian, monarchic primacy of jurisdiction, conceived in an autocratic and absolutist sense. Here is the problem, and it is to the East that we must look for its solution.

The present Pope a few years ago made a significant pilgrimage to the tomb of San Celestino. If he would now resign his see, as did St Celestine, and make it possible for one of the Oriental patriarchs to succeed him, the Latin Church might yet be saved from an ignominious dissolution.

In the meantime, until we are censured for doing so, many of us who have pastoral responsibilities of one kind or another will continue to bear in mind the maxim: "Impossibili nemo tenetur."

The element of Corvine humour in this letter was not appreciated, and probably was not detected, by authority; and some people were puzzled by the letter on account of its concision, not realising that the patriarchs referred to were not members of the Orthodox Church but were Oriental Catholic bishops in communion with the see of Rome. The book which follows is to some extent a commentary on this letter, and aims to show the general reader how it is that a Catholic can differ from the Pope without ceasing to be a Catholic.

The thesis of this book is that at least since the time of St Leo the Great, if not earlier, the papal office has suffered a process of misdevelopment which has had disastrous effects for the Church as a whole, and for the Roman Catholic church itself especially. Providentially, the "Humanae Vitae" affair has now made this so plain that it can only be a matter of time—and let us hope of not very much time—before a remedy is applied. The Catholic Church is sick both *in capite et membris,* and for this reason we look also at the state of the Church's ministry and of its religious orders, both of which are suffering from the general sickness of the body of which they are part. In discussing the ministry it has not seemed necessary to say anything about deacons, since in this country the suggestions of Vatican II for the restoration of the diaconate have not begun to be implemented, so that deacons form no part of the Catholic scene. Being myself in holy orders I have not presumed to write of the laity, who seem to be at the moment the healthiest estate in the Church.

I use the terms "Latin Church" and "Western Church" as denoting both the present-day Catholic Church and the church of the Roman Patriarchate in the early centuries of undivided Christendom.

Similarly the term "Eastern Church", or more accurately "Eastern Churches", is used to denote the present-day Orthodox Church or churches and the "non-Roman" churches of the primitive centuries.

The terms "Catholic" and "Roman Catholic" are used indifferently, and imply no denial of the catholicity of the Orthodox Eastern churches.

The two ecclesiastical provinces of Canterbury and York I regard as being two provinces of the Western Church, though in an anomalous position.

I make no claim to particular learning or scholarship in this field, but merely assert the amateur's right to make the best use that he can of the facts provided by specialists. My debt to the writings of François Dvornik, Gregory Dix, Brian Tierney, John T. Noonan, and others whose names appear in these pages, will be readily apparent.

This book is, of course, in however non-professional a way, a book on theology and church history; and not, basically, a book on religion. A man's religion is the sum of his beliefs concerning God and God's relation to the world and to mankind. For orthodox Christians these beliefs are conveniently summarised in the articles of the Apostles' and the Nicene Creeds. Theology is concerned with the elucidation and interpretation of religious beliefs, and especially, perhaps, with protecting the dogmas or revealed truths of religion from misinterpretation. Those who would propose a religion without theology have not understood what is meant either by religion or by theology. From the moment that the writer of the Fourth Gospel wrote that "The Word was made flesh and dwelt among us" it was inevitable that someone should ask, "Exactly what does that mean?", and that an answer of some kind should be given. The formulating of answers to questions of this kind is the theologian's principal function; but since religion is concerned with the ineffable, such answers as he is able to give cannot be exhaustive, and will always have a certain provisional and tentative character. Religious truths may be "explained" by theologians, but they are *perceived* through faith, which, as St John of the Cross tells us, is, for all its obscurity, a certain kind of knowledge.

Thus the interpretation which theologians of one age place on a particular doctrine, and which proves helpful at that particular time, may be found less satisfactory in a later age. When this happens, new theologians will attempt a new interpretation, taking into full account the merits of the old.

This is the process, or part of the process, that is known as the Development of Doctrine, of which Cardinal Newman is the classical exponent. We see the process at work throughout the course of the Church's history, beginning with the early conciliar definitions concerning the Trinity, and the union in the one Person of Christ of the two Natures, divine and human. Such definitions may be seen as in part the result of a shift of the Catholic consciousness in the apprehension of doctrine. Thus there is a distinct difference of emphasis, stemming from a difference in apprehension, between the patristic way of thinking about the mystery of the eucharist and the later medieval way, which found formal expression in the idea of "transubstantiation", as expressed, for example, in the "Definitio contra Albigenses et Catharos" of the Fourth Lateran Council in 1215.

There is really no cause for surprise that at the present time there is going on within the Church a reconsideration and re-appraisal of the doctrine which recognizes that the bishop of Rome holds a primacy of authority in the Church which is in some way connected with and derived from the association of the Roman bishopric with the Apostle Peter. To equate this process of reappraisal with disloyalty to the Holy See is really to deny the possibility of doctrinal "development", and to put an end to theology as a living discipline.[4]

An indispensable work of reference for the general reader wishing to study more closely the origins of the papal primacy is *Documents Illustrating Papal Authority A.D. 96–454* edited by E. Giles and published by SPCK (1952). The editor's elucidatory notes, which frequently involve mention of the great Roman and Anglican controversialists, such as Chapman, Fortescue, Batiffol, Puller, Denny, Gore, and others, are admirably scholarly and impartial.

Since much of this book is concerned with relations between the Roman Catholic and Eastern Orthodox churches, it may be as well to emphasise that I am well aware that Orthodoxy has problems of its own; but it would be irrelevant to discuss them here. Similarly, urgent though the need is for union between Catholicism and Orthodoxy, not all the obstacles are on the Catholic side. Much depends on the growth of the will to unity among the faithful of both churches, and on patient, persevering prayer and work on both sides.

The opinions expressed in this book are, of course, my own, and commit no one else. For valuable suggestions and criticisms I am indebted to a number of friends with whom I have discussed certain points, or who have been kind enough to read the work in typescript and offer their comments. I am especially grateful for advice and information given by the Reverend John McEvilly (Hieromonk John), Mr Alan Neame, and Mr Roderick M. Bell. I should like also to express my thanks to the distinguished historian who, by my request, acted as *censor deputatus* for the historical sections of this book and enabled me to correct a number of errors and inaccuracies; but it would scarcely be proper to associate him by name with a work so likely to be dubbed "controversial".

I must thank particularly my friend Mrs Andrew Sinclair for saying to me one day, at the height of the turmoil over the encyclical, "My dear Father, won't you explain to us how it is that a Catholic can differ from the Pope?" The present work is can attempt to answer this question.

Finally, to save myself from being labelled either as a "Progressive" or a "Conservative" Catholic, let me firmly identify myself as belonging to the Extreme Centre.

12 *November* 1969   BROCARD SEWELL

NOTE

It is not sufficiently brought out concerning Pope Gregory VII (Hildebrand) in pages 48–50 *infra* that this pope was a devout, charitable man, deeply read in the Scriptures, though of a somewhat summary theological culture. He regarded the papal authority as universal and unlimited, and saw the Pope as charged with the mission to promulgate the decisions of the Father, the Son, and the Holy Ghost, as also those of SS. Peter and Paul. For Hildebrand the Roman Church is God's messenger or oracle to all other bishops and to the faithful. The Pope represents St Peter and is mystically identified with him.

Cf. Gregory VII's letter to the faithful of Lombardy, cited in Fliche et Martin, *Histoire de l Eglise*, vol. 8, p. 63. For the "Dictatus Papae" see the same, volume 8, pp. 79–80.

ONE

SAINT PETER IN
THE NEW TESTAMENT

THE fundamental idea of Catholic church order is that the visible church which is governed by bishops in communion with the Bishop of Rome as chief bishop has a direct continuity with the church of the Apostles which was founded by Jesus Christ, the son of God.

This belief was held by both Eastern and Western Christians in the centuries of the undivided church.

Only those bishops and their churches which enjoyed communion with the Roman Church and its bishop were accepted as catholic and orthodox, and therefore as forming part of the universal church founded by Christ.

Thus St Ambrose, in his funeral sermon for his brother Satyrus, says that when his brother was shipwrecked on the coast of Sardinia in the year 376 he decided to ask for baptism in thanksgiving for his escape. In making this request to the local bishop, Satyrus asked him "whether he was in communion with catholic bishops, that is, with the Church of Rome?"[1]

Exactly the same idea was to be found in England over a thousand years later. In the reign of Queen Mary, when Cardinal Pole reconciled England to the Holy See he directed that certain clergymen who had been ordained according to the new forms of

Edward VI should be deprived of their livings and replaced by "catholick men". These catholic men were priests who had been ordained according to the rite of the Roman *Pontifical.*

The terms "Catholic" and "Roman" were regarded as coterminous. The position of the Pope was still far from being fully defined; but that the Bishop of Rome was in some special sense the successor of St Peter, and endowed with a special responsibility towards the whole flock, was accepted by all Christians, Eastern and Western alike. It might still be debated whether the Pope's primacy was of divine or human origin, and what exactly it comprised; but reverence for the first bishop was so great that perhaps these points seemed academic. St Thomas More died for the primacy of the Pope; but it took him ten years to make up his mind about it. In a letter to Thomas Cromwell he says: "I was myself sometime not of the mind that the primacy of that See should be begun by the institution of God." Earlier, discussing with his friend Bonvisi the growth of heresy in England, More had said that his chief anxiety was over eucharistic doctrine, since he thought the papal primacy was of human origin only, "for the more quietness of the ecclesiastical body". But he added at once that he had spoken without reflection, and asked Bonvisi to come back some days later. He then said: "Alas, Mr Bonvisi, whither was I falling when I made you that answer of the primacy of the Church? I assure you, that opinion alone was enough to make me fall from the rest, for that holdeth up all."[2]

Monsignor Pierre Batiffol, a leading authority on the history of the Early Church, says: "This conscious and effective primacy of Rome is for us, Roman Catholics, the consequence of the promises made by Christ to the apostle Peter; our faith sees in these promises the foundation of the divine right of the papacy."[3]

For Catholics, all proposals for the reunion of separated Christian churches must ultimately include recognition of the primacy of the Bishop of Rome. But if we are asked, "Does acceptance of the primacy of the Pope necessarily mean acceptance of the papacy in all points as it has developed since the separation between the Latin (Roman Catholic) and Eastern (Orthodox) churches?" the answer must be no. Reunion between East and West could *never* be achieved on such terms; it is not necessary that they should even be proposed.

It should be possible for Catholics and Orthodox to reach agreement on the basis of the position accorded to the Bishop of Rome by East and West alike in the centuries of the undivided Church.

This should be acceptable to Anglicans also. Encyclical letters of the Lambeth Conference have often begun with the following words, or some similar formula: "We, Bishops of Christ's Holy Catholic Church, professing the faith of the primitive and un-divided Church, as based on Scripture, defined by the first four General Councils . . ." And the Statute Law of England, as enacted in I Elizabeth I, 36, declares:

> Be it enacted that such persons to whom your Highness, your heirs or successors shall hereafter . . . give authority to have or execute any jurisdiction, power, or authority spiritual . . . shall not in any wise have authority or power to order, determine, or adjudge any matter or cause to be heresy, but only such as heretofore have been determined, ordered, or adjudged to be heresy by the authority of the Canonical Scriptures, or by the first four General Councils.

Acceptance of the first four General Councils involves accep-tance of the papacy, though not in its later development, since the first four General Councils concede, at least tacitly, an evident primacy to the bishop of the Roman Church, albeit the extent and nature of that primacy are undefined.

Classic Anglican divines agree. Thus Archbishop Bramhall (1594–1663) says:[4]

> And now, reader, take a look about thee; see among all these branches of papal power which were cast out of England if thou canst find either of St Peter's Keys or his Primacy of Order or his beginning of Unity, or anything which is purely spiritual, that hath no further influences than merely the court of con-science.

Bishop Lancelot Andrewes (1555–1626) says in his *Responsio ad Bellarminum* (Reply to Cardinal Bellarmine):

> Neither is it questioned among us whether St Peter had a primacy, but what that primacy was; and whether it were such an one as the Pope doth now challenge to himself and you challenge to the Pope; but the King doth not deny Peter to have been the Prime and Prince of the Apostles.

A recent Anglican writer, Dr Trevor Jalland, says in his book *The Church and the Papacy: a Historical Study*:[5]

> . . . the evidences of the first three centuries appear to show that *in fact* the Roman see was regarded as in some sense a centre of reference, particularly in matters of doctrine, but also on occasion in those which concerned discipline as well, and that when the question began to be asked why this was so, non-Roman as well as Roman Christians usually replied that it was due to the connexion of that see with St Peter as one of its co-founders.

It might be thought, on the evidence, that Dr Jalland's cautious words "appear to show" are an understatement.

But before looking at the evidence of the first three centuries it is necessary to look at the evidence of the New Testament concerning the relationship between Christ and St Peter and between St Peter and the other Apostles. For it is the belief of Catholics that the papal primacy is a scriptural doctrine, in the sense that its origin and roots are to be found in scripture.

Lists of the names of the Apostles occur in the three Synoptic Gospels (Matthew, Mark, Luke) and in the Acts of the Apostles. Peter's name always comes first, and Judas Iscariot's last.

Peter is the regular spokesman for the other Apostles. He is mentioned altogether in the New Testament 195 times; the rest of the Apostles 130 times. This means that Peter is mentioned considerably more often than all the other Apostles taken together.

The next in order of mention is St John, the "beloved disciple", who is mentioned 29 times; that is, about seven times less than St Peter.

St Matthew (x, 2), beginning his list of Apostles, says: "Now the names of the twelve apostles are these: The first, Simon, who is called Peter. . . ." The word "first" seems to indicate clearly a special dignity. As his name is first in the list it is scarcely necessary to describe Peter as "the first" "unless his position at the head was a statutory chairmanship ordained by the Master who had called and ordained the Twelve."[6]

In the controversy over the question of whether converts to the new Christian faith should be obliged to conform to the Jewish practice of circumcision or not, Paul and Barnabas were deputed to go up to Jerusalem to consult "the apostles and elders" on the matter (Acts xv). After much discussion at this specially convened meeting St Peter rises and decides the matter authoritatively, saying: "Brethren, ye know how that a good while ago God made choice among you that by my mouth the Gentiles should hear the word of the gospel and believe." After which, "all the multitude kept silence". St James, the local bishop, then rose to speak in support of Peter's decision; but unlike St Peter he did not speak from a special position of authority, and began by asking to be heard ("Men, brethren, hear me"). St Peter's pronouncement was accepted as authoritative and irresistible.

St Paul's reproof of St Peter is recorded in Galatians ii as if it were something very extraordinary that the last and least of the Apostles, who had not been with the Lord in the days of his flesh, should correct the first. Paul was right to denounce Peter for going back on his earlier principles, not eating with Gentiles out of fear of the Jewish Christian reactionary party; but he does not denounce him by appealing to any other or higher authority; he reproves him for inconsistency with his own known and publicly professed principles.

In spite of the way it has been overworked by Catholics, the most striking testimony of all to St Peter's special position and privileges is the passage in Matthew xvi, 17–19, where Christ asks his Apostles, collectively, "But who do you say that I am?", and

Peter, speaking for them all, answers: "Thou art the Christ, the Son of the living God." Then:

> Jesus answered and said to him, Blessed art thou, Simon Bar-Jona, for flesh and blood hath not revealed it to thee, but my Father which is in heaven. And I myself say to thee that thou art Rock, and on this rock I will build my church, and the gates of Hades shall not prevail against it. And I will give thee the keys of the kingdom of heaven, and whatsoever thou shalt bind on earth shall be bound in heaven, and whatsoever thou shalt loose on earth shall be loosed in heaven.

In the course of two articles on "St Peter in the New Testament"[7] the Anglican scholar C. H. Turner, then Ireland Professor of New Testament Exegesis at Oxford, wrote:

> Let me say, to start with, that I think we of the Church of England and Protestant scholars in general since the Reformation have failed to give its due weight to the testimony supplied by the New Testament, and in particular by the Gospels, to the unique position there ascribed to St Peter.
>
> Protestants have been under an overwhelming temptation to minimise anything in the New Testament which might seem to give the beginnings of the Roman theory of the Papacy; Anglicans have been so anxious to bring into strong relief the unique position of the Apostles that they have tended to overlook any parallel indications of a unique position amongst the Apostles of St Peter. . . .
>
> What impresses me more than anything else is the convergence of the testimony of these four documents [the four Gospels] in the prerogative position allotted to St Peter. The writers are not simply repeating one another; the more important sayings are different, the indications to all appearance independent; but they cohere to a remarkable degree, and they must, I think, be taken to represent the common attitude of all parts and sections of the Christian society in its earliest stages.

Commenting in the same article on Matthew xvi, 17–19, Dr Turner continues:

In the circles from which the matter peculiar to the First Gospel was drawn, the prerogative position of St Peter was amply recognised. But there remains, of course, still to consider the most striking testimony of all. . . . And I myself say to thee that thou art ROCK and on this ROCK I will build my Church, and the gates of Hades shall not prevail against it. . . .

No words could well be more startling than these. In the Palestinian surroundings where the First Gospel was put into shape, no sort of doubt can have existed as to the unique position conferred by Christ on his chief Apostle; and if for Palestinian we substitute "Syrian" or "Antiochene", we must ascribe the belief to Gentile as well as to Jewish Christians. Even if the belief were not based on fact, it was quite definitely held within the first fifty years of the life of the Christian Society. . . . I think we shall find reason to suspect that no such promise was made to the Apostle on the occasion to which St Matthew ascribes it; but I think we shall also find reason to conjecture that some such promise was really uttered by our Lord at a later and still more supreme moment.

Of these words of Professor Turner, Father Vincent McNabb says: "Leaving to Catholic exegetes, therefore, the question whether the context of Matt. xvi is chronologically exact, we are content to insist that whatever view may be finally accepted about the place and time of these words of Jesus to Peter, there can be no doubt that they convey not merely a *privilege*, but a *primacy*."

The contemporary Protestant theologian Oscar Cullman asks[8] concerning the same passage from Matthew xvi: "Can this saying have been spoken by Jesus, or was it only created by the Church after his death?" The only reason for questioning its authenticity would seem to be the suggestion that Jesus, who spent his public ministry in preaching the coming *Kingdom* of God, would not have spoken of a *Church*. But earlier critics, among them Strauss and Bauer, accepted the text as genuine, as did Albert Schweitzer, who identified the Church with the Kingdom of God conceived of eschatologically. Other Protestant biblical scholars (Kattenbusch, K. L. Schmidt, and others) think that Jesus could only have spoken of a church in the meaning that the word (Hebrew *qahal*) would have had for a Jew of Christ's time; that is, a people of saints, or the people of God. A Catholic need have no difficulty in accepting this view.

As Cullmann puts it: "We must emphasise that the Greek word for Church, *ekklesia*, does not designate anything like a Christian creation, but belongs to the Jewish sphere." So the well-known phrase might be accurately re-translated as "On this rock I will build my people of God".

Cullmann sums up by saying that "all Protestant interpretations that seek in one way or another to explain away the reference to Peter seem to me unsatisfactory. No, the fact remains that when Jesus says he will build his *ekklesia* upon this Rock, he really means the person of Simon."

But other interpretations have been held at different times even by Catholics, such as the idea of the *rock* being Peter's faith rather than his person. Catholic controversialists have not always been justified in labelling such interpretations as "Protestant". Today, however, the best exegetes, both Catholic and Protestant, seem agreed that the identification of Simon Peter himself with the Rock is the only one that is possible.

Protestant and Catholic now seem basically at one as to the meaning of the whole passage. Thus Cullmann writes:

> In Matthew 16:19 it is presupposed that Christ is the master of the house, who has the keys to the kingdom of heaven, with which to open to those who come in. Just as in Isaiah 22:22 the Lord lays the keys of the house of David on the shoulders of his servant Eliakim, so Jesus commits to Peter the keys of his house, the Kingdom of Heaven, and thereby installs him as administrator of the house.

Father McNabb says:

> This primacy has functions described by two words: Rock, and Key-bearer. The function of a Rock is static rather than dynamic. Only a Rock gives an immoveable foundation to the house, as St Matthew himself records (vii, 24–25). But when the

house is built and dwelt in there must be a key and a key-bearer to make the in-dwellers safe. St Peter is not merely the Rock, but he is equally the key-bearer. His primacy begins with the beginning and continues to the end! No other Apostle has a function comparable to this. *Indeed, the truth is that no other individual Apostle is given any official function.*

Note that while St Peter certainly shares the power of binding and loosing with the other Apostles (Matthew xviii, 18), he is the only one to whom this commission is given individually, and the only one to whom the "keys" are committed. While the exercise of this power of binding and loosing is evidently intended to be in some sense corporate, or collegial as we should say today, it is assigned to Peter, as it is not to any of the other Apostles, individually—by name.

Having given St Peter this primacy, or position of special responsibility and authority, in his Church, Christ later, both by word and action, showed him how this authority was to be exercised. St Luke describes in his twenty-second chapter how after the Last Supper

there arose also a contention among them [the Apostles], which of them is to be accounted the greatest. And [Jesus] said unto them: The kings of the Gentiles have lordship over them; and they that have authority over them are called Benefactors. But ye shall not be so: but he that is the greater among you, let him become as the younger; and he that is chief, as he that serveth. For whether is greater, he that sitteth at meat, or he that serveth? is not he that sitteth at meat? but I am in the midst of you as he that serveth. But ye are they which have continued with me in my temptations; and I appoint unto you a kingdom, even as my Father appointed unto me, that ye may eat and drink at my table in my kingdom; and ye shall sit on thrones, judging the twelve tribes of Israel.

Simon, Simon, behold, Satan asked to have you, that he might sift you as wheat; but I have prayed for thee that thy faith fail not: and do thou, when once thou hast turned again, stablish thy brethren.

Here the Apostles are told, in oriental imagery, that they are appointed to administer Christ's kingdom, but that, unlike earthly rulers, they are not to lord it over those committed to their care, but are to serve them, just as they themselves have been served by Christ, their lord and master. The words "He that is the greater among you, let him become as the younger, and he that is chief as he that serveth" must have had a special significance for St Peter, to whom the closing words of the discourse again assign a special place. Satan, Christ says, has sought to "have" you, the Apostles (the word "you" here is plural); but Christ has prayed for Peter singly, so that *his* faith may not fail; and when he is re-established in grace after his coming fall (the denial of his Master in Pilate's judgement hall) it will be his special work to strengthen his brethren in the apostolic college.

These words form part of Christ's solemn farewell charge to the Twelve—though Judas had left by then—after the Last Supper. St John tells us (ch. xiii, 4–10) how after the Supper Jesus girded himself with a towel and washed the feet of his disciples, addressing a particular admonition to Peter. Then, addressing all the Apostles, he said: "Know ye what I have done to you? Ye call Me Lord and Master, and ye say well; for so I am. If I then, the Lord and Master, have washed your feet, ye also ought to wash one another's feet. For I have given you an example, that ye also should do as I have done unto you."

In the Fourth Gospel almost the last recorded words of Jesus are concerned with Peter. The scene is early in the morning on the shore of the sea of Galilee, after the Resurrection. Peter and six other disciples have just returned from a night's fishing. The Lord is waiting for them on the beach, where he has made a fire and cooked a breakfast for them. ("I am among you as he that serveth.") After the meal

Jesus saith to Simon Peter, Simon, son of John, lovest thou me more than these? He said unto him, Yea, Lord; thou knowest that I love thee. He said unto him, Feed my lambs. He saith to him again a second time, Simon, son of John, lovest thou me? He saith unto him, Yea, Lord, thou knowest that I love thee.

He saith unto him, Tend my sheep. He saith unto him the third time, Simon, son of John, lovest thou me? Peter was grieved because he said unto him the third time, Lovest thou me? And he said unto him, Lord, thou knowest all things; thou knowest that I love thee. Jesus saith unto him, Feed my sheep.

In his Commentary on St John's Gospel, Westcott[9] says that "The representative official precedence of St Peter thus really underlies the whole narrative of the fourth Gospel." There is an interesting comment on this passage from John xxi in a posthumously published work[10] by the Tractarian divine William Sewell, sometime Fellow of Exeter College and Professor of Moral Philosophy at Oxford. Dr Sewell points out that the Greek word *arnía* used for sheep or lambs in v. 15 ("Feed my lambs") probably means sheep regarded individually and not collectively; while the word *boske* ("Feed") means give them food or pasture. Thus "Our Lord's first charge to Peter is the Pastoral Office of the Church— the preaching of the Word, the administering of the Sacraments: the Cure of Souls."

After Peter's reply to his second questioning by Christ ("Lovest thou me?"), Christ says: "Tend my sheep" (v. 16): in the Greek *poimaine ta probatá mou*; which Dr Sewell translates as "Be the shepherd of my flocks". On this sentence he says:

The difference between the verb now used and the former is that the former implies the performance of all the duties of a shepherd, including especially those of government, direction, and discipline. And *probatá*, flocks, is not the same as *arnía*, sheep individually: it means the flocks, and perhaps herds also, all feeding together, *advancing forward*, moving onwards in a body. . . . In this second charge is given the spiritual supervision and government of the Church.

Coming to the third commission (v. 17), "Feed my sheep (Greek *Boske ta probatía mou* in certain codices):

Boske is again substituted for *poimaine* and *probatía* takes the place of *probatá* . . . *probatía* may mean little flocks; but it may also bear the signification of "pasture grounds for flocks", and from this it would refer to a number of flocks in different pastures. The flock of Christ in a single parish would thus be represented by *arnía*, the flock of Christ gathered in one diocese under its Bishop by the second *probatá*, and the whole Catholic Church, feeding, as it were, in many distinct pasturages, would be implied by the third word *probatía*.

Christ's commission *here* is to *feed* the flock (*boskein* but not *poimainein*), not to obtrude upon it the other duties of a shepherd. How hard indeed it is to draw this line! very hard for a Church which realises all its own blessings, its preservation of the Faith, its close relationship to Jesus Christ. It is extremely difficult for such a Church, when stretching out assistance to others less blessed, to hold its hands and check itself from interference in the Church government of others.

This piece of exegesis is remarkable in what it concedes as coming from one who was strongly, if not violently, opposed to the claims of the Church of Rome.[11]

When one has read and studied carefully all the New Testament references to St Peter it is very hard to see how Bishop Gore could say,[12] "If you read the New Testament as a whole, you see that the idea of any official authority being given to St Peter over and above what was given to the rest of the Apostles has no support at all."

Bishop Lightfoot[13] thought otherwise. Writing about St Clement of Rome in his edition of *The Apostolic Fathers* Lightfoot says:

Even a cursory glance at the history of the Apostles, so far as it appears in the Gospel records, reveals a certain primacy of St Peter among the twelve. He holds the first place in all lists; he has a precedence of responsibility and temptation; he sets the example of moral courage and of moral lapse. Above all, he receives special pastoral charges. . . . Peter asserts his primacy in the foundation of the Christian Church . . . he takes the initiative at all the great crises of development. . . . The greatest conquest of all still awaited him. The Church must become a world-wide Church. . . . By virtue of his primacy Peter is chosen as the recipient of this revelation of revelations.

TWO

THE CHAIR OF PETER

THE primacy of Peter among the other Apostles admits of no doubt. It is equally clear that the primacy was given to him because of his profession of the true faith in Christ, and that the meaning of the primacy must be interpreted in the light of this fact. Was this primacy granted to Peter intended by Christ to be continued after Peter's death in a line of successors until the end of time? Roman Catholic apologists claim that it was; but there is nothing in the Gospels or other New Testament writings that says so. Catholic divines commonly argue that a continuance of the primacy was fitting, and morally necessary for the building up and unification of the infant church. But the argument from "fittingness" is the weakest of all theological arguments, being invoked usually in defence of points of doctrine for which there is little or no evidence either in scripture or history. A continuance of the primacy would indeed seem to have been fitting; but this is no proof that it was intended.

However, the argument against the continued primacy from the silence of scripture is not conclusive. Argument from silence is almost as precarious as argument from fittingness. There is no scriptural evidence that Christ intended the rite which he inaugurated at the Last Supper ("Do this in memory of me") to be continued after the death of those to whom these words were addressed, and until the end of time. Yet the Church has been conscious almost from the first that this was her Founder's intention.

Some kind of general supervisory authority and centre of reference was morally necessary for the multiplying communities of the early Christian church, and almost from its foundation the Roman church began to fill this rôle, which was accepted by other churches chiefly because of the special connexion of that church with Peter. Undoubtedly the Roman church's special position as the church of the capital of the Roman Empire was a factor in the special prestige enjoyed by that church; and being in the capital, the church there enjoyed a special ease of communication with other places. But these factors hardly account for the special status of the Roman church before the Emperor Constantine made Christianity the Empire's official religion. A mass of evidence—among it inscriptions in the Roman catacombs—shows that the early Roman church was intensely conscious of having been founded by the Apostles Peter and Paul, and especially of its connexion with Peter, the Prince of the Apostles.

The Roman church seems to have exercised a distinct, though undefined, primacy towards other churches from the moment it was sufficiently organised to be able to do so. The first clear example of this is the *First Epistle of Clement to the Corinthians*. Batiffol, in his *Primitive Catholicism*, speaks of this letter as "the epiphany of the Roman primacy". It was written probably towards the end of the year 96. St Clement, "who beheld the Apostles"—that is, Peter and Paul—was only the third bishop of Rome after St Peter. His letter was written with the aim of healing the dissensions that had broken out in the church at Corinth, and it appears to have been a spontaneous and unsolicited intervention. News travelled quickly in the Roman Empire. The disturbance in the church at Corinth must surely have been known in Ephesus, which was much nearer than Rome. Why was there no intervention from the church at Ephesus, which was probably still presided over by the last surviving Apostle?

Clement's latest translator and editor[1] says that the epistle contains "no suggestion that any prescriptive authority inheres as yet in the Roman Church itself". Yet the tone of the letter is one of quiet self-confidence, as when, in his first paragraph, the writer refers to "the odious and unholy breach of unity among you, and which a few hot-headed and unruly individuals have inflamed to such a pitch that your venerable and illustrious name, so richly deserving of everyone's affection, has been brought into serious disrepute". There is a note of authority too in the postscript also, where Clement says: "Make haste and send our messengers, Claudius Ephebus, Valerius Vito, and Fortunatus, back to us in peace and joy; so that the news of the truce and unity for which we pray and long may reach us the more speedily, and we may the sooner rejoice over your return to order."

In Claudius, Valerius, and Fortunatus we may recognise the first papal legates. However, the letter contains no specific claim of the Roman church to special authority; the exchanging of pastoral letters was a common practice in the sub-apostolic age. Perhaps the most that can be said is that the special dignity of the Roman church as the church of Peter seems to have been taken for granted by other churches, as something well known. As Batiffol says,[2] "the Roman primacy has none of the features of a high-handed conquest . . .; the evidence of its existence comes to us in the form of acknowledgements of it by others more often than as claims set up by Rome."

Batiffol also says[3] that "the Catholicism of the first centuries manifests itself as a communion of innumerable churches distributed throughout the world; a communion at once mystical and concrete, founded on unity of faith and institutions, and having as its perceptible centre of gravity the Roman Church. It has been said that 'all the elements of the later evolution of the Church are ready at the end of the second century, and even earlier, except for the Christian emperor. . . . Even the *de facto* primacy of Rome is already undeniable.' " (The quotation is from the Protestant scholar Adolf Harnack.)

No one seriously disputes today that the Roman church had a consciousness of pre-eminence practically from the beginning; but until the fourth century the bishops of Rome did not particularly emphasise their primacy, nor was any attempt made to define it.

The primacy can be allowed only a very restricted significance at this time. The earliest witnesses show that it was bound up with the association of the Apostles Peter and Paul with the city of Rome. There is the well known passage of St Irenaeus (*c.* 130–*c.* 200):

> Those who wish to know the truth may observe the apostolic tradition made manifest in every church throughout the world. We can enumerate those who were appointed bishops in the churches by the Apostles and their successors down to our own days. . . . But as it would be excessively lengthy . . . to enumerate the succession in all the churches we do so by pointing to the apostolic tradition and the faith that is preached to all men, which has come down to us through the successions of the bishops; the tradition and creed of the greatest, the most ancient church, the church known to all men, which was founded and set up at Rome by the two most glorious Apostles, Peter and Paul. For with this church, because of its superior origin, it is necessary that every other church should be in communion—that is, the faithful everywhere; for in her the apostolic tradition has always been preserved by the faithful from all parts.[4]

Irenaeus, who was himself bishop of Lyons, does not name either Peter or Paul as the first bishop of Rome, but says that the two founders installed Linus as bishop, noting that St Paul mentions Linus in his epistles to Timothy (2 Tim. iv, 21). He gives the succession after Linus as Anacletus, Clement, Evaristus, Alexander, Sixtus, Telesphorus, Hyginus, Pius, Anicetus, Soter, and Eleutherius ("who now occupies the see"). Irenaeus's remarks about Clement are of particular interest. He says that Clement "not only saw the blessed Apostles but also conferred with them, and had their preaching ringing in his ears and their tradition before his eyes. . . . Now while Clement was bishop there arose no small dissension among the brethren in Corinth, and the Church in Rome sent a most weighty letter to the Corinthians urging them to reconciliation, renewing their faith, and telling them again of the tradition which he lately received from the Apostles."

Eusebius (*c.* 260–*c.* 340), bishop of Caesaria and the Father of Church History, lists in his *Ecclesiastical History* Peter and Paul as founders at Rome; Peter at Antioch; and Mark at Alexandria. Alexandria has always been recognised as an "apostolic" see, perhaps because of St Mark's close association with St Paul (Acts xii, xiii, xv) and with St Peter (1 Peter, v, 13). Like Irenaeus, Eusebius does not include the names of the founders of these churches in the lists of their bishops. Contrary to modern Roman Catholic tendency, bishops can never be identified in a literal sense as "successors of the Apostles", for the rôle of the Apostle was unique, and his office surpassed in every way that of a bishop. The Apostles were, generally speaking, itinerant missionaries. When an Apostle founded a local church he appointed and consecrated a minister (bishop) to reside there and care for the church. The Apostle then moved on to another area to establish a church and bishop there also. To speak of St Peter as the first bishop of Rome is not strictly accurate.

From the beginning the Church arranged its administration in conformity with the political divisions of the Roman empire.[5] This arrangement was due to the Apostles themselves. Key cities in this respect, besides Rome, were Antioch, the capital of Syria; Ephesus, the capital of the province of Asia; Alexandria, the capital of Egypt, Libya, and Pentapolis; and Jerusalem, the capital of Palestine. Each of the churches established in these cities was, directly or indirectly, of apostolic foundation, and had a special dignity for that reason; but their locations were chosen in the first place as being provincial capitals. Rome was the only apostolic see in the West; nevertheless, it was recognised as having a special dignity and authority, for which there was no equivalent in the East. Rome's position as capital of the Empire is not enough to explain this pre-eminence of the Roman church. It is clear that a special *mystique* attached to the Roman See because of its connexion with St Peter. Naturally, when the Emperor removed from Rome to Constantinople at the beginning of the fourth century a new emphasis on the position of the Pope developed in the West, but essentially it derived from the original *mystique*, which must have come from apostolic tradition.

In the year 312 the Emperor Constantine the Great placed Christianity on a level with other recognised cults in the Empire, and later it was raised to a privileged position. It was his policy to unite the Church with the State by the closest possible ties. The Emperor regarded himself, and was regarded, as virtually a vice-regent of Christ, with the right and duty of watching over the Church and all Christian people. This way of looking at things derived from the hellenistic political thought that was then current in the East. In particular, the Emperor claimed that the right of convoking ecumenical councils belonged to him.

Ecumenical, or General, Councils were assemblies of bishops of the universal church, together with other members of the clergy. (The laity was often represented by others besides the Emperor.) Definitions of doctrine and disciplinary decrees passed by general councils were considered binding on all Christians. Where definitions of doctrine were concerned it was believed that the Holy Ghost would protect such definitions from error. The early councils were summoned by the Emperor; their ecumenical status derived from their general recognition by the Church as a whole, from the position accorded to them in the early canonical collections, and from the usage of the schools (of theology). Later, the Gregorian canonists advanced a theory, which won acceptance in the West, that for validity and binding force the decrees of Councils required at least tacit acceptance by the papacy.

Catholics and Orthodox alike regard the doctrinal decrees of ecumenical councils as of supreme authority; but they differ considerably in the number of councils which they recognise as ecumenical.

Article XXI of the Church of England's Articles of Religion says that things ordained by general councils as necessary to salvation "have neither strength nor authority unless it may be declared that they be taken out of Holy Scripture". This formula seems to be capable of conciliation with the Catholic and Orthodox view of councils; in any case, as we have seen, Anglicans accept the first four (if not six) general councils as authoritative. Generally speaking, however, the first seven Councils (Nicaea, Constantinople, Ephesus, Chalcedon, Constantinople II and III, and Nicaea II) are reckoned as ecumenical by Orthodox, Catholics, and Anglicans. But since the official formularies of the Church of England seem to recognise only the first four, these are the ones that need to be considered in order to determine what was the attitude of the primitive undivided church to the prerogatives of the Bishop of Rome.

The First Council of Nicaea was held in the year 325. It was summoned by the Emperor Constantine, principally to deal with the doctrines, subsequently judged to be heretical, of the priest Arius. The acts of the Council are not extant, all that survives being the Council's formulation of the Creed, the synodal letter, and twenty canons. Three hundred and eighteen bishops are supposed to have attended. Its membership was almost entirely Eastern. The only representatives from the West were Hosius, the bishop of Cordova (who according to some accounts acted as president after the Emperor's opening speech), the bishops of Carthage, Milan, Dijon, and two others. The Bishop of Rome was represented by two priests.

The first to sign the acts of the Council were the Western bishop Hosius and the two priest-representatives of the Holy See. This speaks for itself as a general indication of the special position accorded by the assembly to the Roman church. Canon 6 of the Council of Nicaea said:

> Let the old customs have force which exist in Egypt and Libya and the Pentapolis, so that the Bishop of Alexandria should have authority over all these [provinces], inasmuch as that is also the custom of the Bishop of Rome; and that likewise about Antioch and in the other provinces their ancient rights should be preserved to the churches.

This canon was concerned with the status of metropolitan sees; the example of Rome was regarded as authoritative, and the canon was constantly appealed to later in support of Roman jurisdictional claims. It says nothing, however, about the primacy of the Bishop of Rome, with which it was not concerned. The Roman bishop is referred to simply as a metropolitan with several ecclesiastical provinces under his jurisdiction.

The First Council of Constantinople (381) was convoked by the Emperor Theodosius to unite the Church on the basis of the Nicene faith at the end of the Arian controversy. Canon 3 of this council enacted "that the Bishop of Constantinople have the privilege of honour after the Bishop of Rome, because it [Constantinople] is the New Rome."

This granting of the second place in the hierarchy was made principally because of the Emperor's residence at Constantinople; later it came to be held that Constantinople was an "apostolic" see since it incorporated the extinct see of Ephesus. The canon was not aimed in any way at diminishing the special position of the Bishop of Rome. It encountered no opposition in the East, and none in the West for another seventy years.

The Council of Ephesus (431) was summoned by the Emperor Theodosius II to settle the Nestorian controversy. The history and acts of this Council show that all those present, most of whom were Easterns, acknowledged that Rome is the "apostolic see" *par excellence*, because it is the see of Peter; that Peter held the primacy in the Church; that Celestine, the reigning Pope, was St Peter's successor; and that in virtue of this succession Celestine was able to depose a Patriarch of Constantinople, and to declare to all what was the orthodox faith.

In the course of the second session the Pope's legate, the bishop Projectus, addressing the assembly, said:

> Let your holinesses consider the form of the writings of the holy and venerable pope Celestine, the bishop, who has exhorted your holinesses [not as if teaching the ignorant, but as reminding them that know] that those things which he had long ago defined, and now thought it right to remind you of, ye might give command to be carried out to the uttermost, according to the canon of the common faith, and according to the use of the Catholic church.

After the Pope's letter had been read, the legates asked the Council to ratify it, which seems to show that, in spite of the immense spiritual authority allowed to the bishop of Rome, those present recognised the Council as the supreme and final authority, whose decisions cannot be questioned.

The Council of Chalcedon (451) was summoned by the Emperor Marcian to deal with the heresy of Eutyches. At the first session there were from five to six hundred bishops present, all of them Easterns except two from Africa and the two papal legates, Paschasinus and Boniface.

Canon 28 confirmed canon 3 of Ephesus and placed certain territories of Asia Minor and Europe under the jurisdiction of Constantinople. The canon reads as follows:

> Adhering in all things to the decisions of the holy Fathers, and acknowledging the canon . . . of the 150 bishops [of the council of Constantinople] . . . we also do enact and decree the same things concerning the privileges of the most holy church of Constantinople, which is New Rome. For the Fathers rightly granted privileges to the throne of old Rome, because it was the royal city. And the 150 most religious bishops, actuated by the same consideration, gave equal privileges to the most holy throne of New Rome, justly judging that the city which is honoured with the sovereignty and the senate, and enjoys equal privileges with the old imperial Rome, should in ecclesiastical matters also be magnified as she is, and rank next after her . . .[6]

This is certainly an awkward text for those who defend an extreme view of papal authority. The historian Hefele, himself a Catholic and a bishop, says on page 428 of the third volume of his *History of General Councils*: "How it is possible to imagine for an instant that the bishops of this Council considered the rights they were discussing to be of divine origin, and that the occupant of the See of Rome was, *jure divino*, supreme over all pontiffs, I cannot understand." But Hefele later subscribed to the Decrees of the Vatican Council of 1870.

This canon, which ascribes a *civil* origin to the special status of the Roman See, drew, later, a sharp protest from the Bishop of Rome, St Leo the Great, to the Bishop of Constantinople, Anatolius, whom he rebuked for transgressing the canons of Nicaea, which had established the correct order of precedence.

The new arrangement, sanctioned by canon 3 of Ephesus, had, the Pope declared, deprived the see of Alexandria of its second place in the hierarchy, and Antioch of its position as the third. Moreover, in the territories newly subjected to Constantinople by Chalcedon the metropolitans had been deprived of their rights. A similar protest was sent by the Pope to the Empress Pulcheria Augusta.[7]

However, the fact that the Emperor, the Patriarch of Constantinople, and the Fathers of the Council of Chalcedon all wished the Pope to accept this canon shows that none of them saw in it any threat to the Pope's position in the church.

It is with St Leo the Great that the papal claims specifically reach the form which we may identify as "Roman Catholic", in the sense that they go beyond the primacy which Eastern Christians of the early centuries were willing to recognise as belonging to the Bishop of Rome, and have since proved equally unacceptable to Protestant Christians of later centuries. Leo, who was Pope from the year 440 until his death in 461, advanced and strengthened the authority of the Roman see to an enormous extent. He was deeply convinced that the supremacy of his see was founded on divine and scriptural authority, and was of universal extent. His greatest triumph was the acceptance by the Council of Chalcedon, at which his legates presided, of the document known as The Tome of Leo, a statement of doctrine to be used as the test of Christological orthodoxy. This letter, also called "Epistola Dogmatica", had originally been sent by the Pope two years previously to Flavian, the Patriarch of Constantinople. The Council of Chalcedon gave it formal authority as the classical exposition of the Catholic doctrine of the Incarnation, and its reading was greeted at the Council by the acclamation "Peter has spoken through Leo".

This seems to show that the idea of the Pope as a kind of oracle, and reincarnation of Peter the Apostle, was already, in practice, widely held. No one, of course, would have expressed themselves formally in this way; it was more a question of an ethos, that is, a characteristic spirit or way of looking at things.

Leo was a clear and forcible writer, whose sermons can move

the reader even today. A typical example of his style, a simple, vigorous Latinity, is the well known first lesson in the second nocturn of the Roman Breviary's office of Matins for Christmas. In his *The Life and Times of St Leo the Great* Trevor Jalland says that "The Vatican Constitution of 1870, *De Ecclesia Christi*, assigns a twofold Primacy to the Roman See, one of Jurisdiction and one of Doctrine. It may perhaps be admitted that it is not until the appearance of the Fourth Tractate of Gelasius I that we find a clear and unequivocal assertion of the former. Yet it is beyond any possibility of doubt that we owe to Leo I the earliest affirmation of the Doctrinal Primacy, an affirmation which was widely accepted or conceded by churches in the East as well as in the West."

Leo believed that what distinguished the authority of St Peter from that of the other apostles was precisely its *universality*, which he saw as conferred by Christ in his charge to Peter recorded in John xxi, 15–17. In his letters Leo uses this text to justify his intervention in the affairs of other churches (in Sicily, Spain, Gaul, Africa, etc.), and to vindicate the Pope's right to overrule local customs. Leo regarded himself as having the direct and immediate care of all churches, by divine appointment. For him, the authority of other bishops amounts to a share in his own authority, and is received only through himself as Peter's successor.

He held that the Pope is the personal representative and visible embodiment of Peter—ideas which Jalland says can be traced back to Pope Siricius—and to him the Petrine privileges were a sacred charge to be jealously protected. His Tome claims explicitly that the Roman see is the final authority in matters of doctrine because of its connexion with St Peter; yet the universal authority of the Tome itself was clearly conferred on it by the Council of Chalcedon, for no council would have ratified a papal document had not its contents been in accord with both Scripture and Apostolic Tradition. There is no question but that popes are capable of putting forward, publicly, doctrinal statements of doubtful orthodoxy, and therefore there must be a higher authority capable of condemning such statements. Two of the most famous papal blunders of this kind are the Arian formula subscribed to in the year 357 by Pope Liberius and the virtually Monothelite doctrine proposed by Honorius I. For this Honorius was actually condemned by the Council of Constantinople of 681. These two instances of papal fallibility, while perhaps technically conciliable with the doctrine of infallibility of 1870, afford ample justification for the widespread anxiety within the papal church today over the soundness of the doctrine expressed in the encyclical "Humanae Vitae".

The first tensions between the Eastern and Western Churches were concerned with different theories of ecclesiastical organisation, the East, roughly speaking, basing itself on imperial territorial division, the West on the principle of apostolic foundation. East and West both admitted the Roman primacy, but they advanced different theories to explain its origin.

In the year 482 Pope Felix excommunicated the Patriarch of Constantinople, Acacius, because of certain concessions he was alleged to have made to the Monophysites; and ten years later Pope Gelasius repudiated canon 28 of Chalcedon, and refused to Constantinople even the status of a metropolitan city. The strong line taken by Gelasius is of great significance for the future development of the papacy. He denounced the Emperor's right to intervene in religious matters at all, which was a complete break with ancient custom and with the hellenistic thought that had prevailed up to that time.

The Pope was probably right in this matter; the granting of second place to Constantinople in the year 381 was certainly less than just to the apostolic see of Alexandria, which was demoted to third place. But the Holy See had accepted this at the time, and for a pope a century later to make the matter a *casus belli* was injudicious, to say the least. Gelasius had rejected the traditional hellenistic view of the relations between Church and State, and the fact that he so strenuously exalted the rôle of the clergy and placed the Church *above* the State sowed the seeds of serious misdevelopments in the Western Church, which would grow up and bear unexpected fruit after the separation of the West from the East.

"Two things", Gelasius told the Emperor, "govern the world: the sacred authority of the pontiff and the imperial power. Of these two, the priests bear a greater burden inasmuch as at the Judgement they will have to render an account not only for themselves, but also for kings."[8]

The affair of Acacius led to a schism between East and West which lasted from 484–519. It was ended by Pope Hormisdas and the Emperor Justinian. The Eastern bishops all signed the *Libellus Hormisdae*, a document which gave emphatic emphasis to the Roman primacy, as follows:

The first thing necessary for salvation is to keep the rule of the true faith and in no wise to swerve from the constitutions of the Fathers. And because it is not possible to set aside the saying of our Lord Jesus Christ: Thou art Peter, and on this rock I will build my church, these words are verified by the facts, because it is in the apostolic see that the catholic faith has always been preserved without stain. . . . We receive and approve the encyclical letters of blessed Leo our Pope on the Christian religion,[9] . . . following in all things the holy see and preaching everything that it ordains. And above all things I hope to be found worthy to be in the one communion with yourself, as the holy see enjoins, for in this consists the entire, true, and perfect stability of the Christian religion. And I promise for the time to come not to remember in the sacred mysteries the names of those sequestrated from the communion of the Catholic Church: that is, those who are not in communion with the apostolic see.[10]

The signing of this document by the Eastern bishops was a clear admission on their part of the primacy of the Holy See, and seemed to imply that the Holy See was the bond and centre of Christian unity *jure divino*.

The reconciliation between East and West was principally the work of the Emperor Justinian, who issued a series of remarkable "novellae" or edicts regulating the relationship between Church and State. In Novella 6, of March 6th 535, he wrote:[11]

The greatest gifts that God, in his infinite bounty, has made to men are the *sacerdotium* and the *imperium*. The priesthood takes care of the divine interests, the empire of the human interests with which it is charged. Both of them spring from the same source and lead human life to its perfection. That is why the emperors have nothing more at heart than to honour priests, who pray continually to God for the emperor. When the clergy has a good spirit and trusts entirely in God, when the emperor governs the commonweal that is confided to him, then there results a harmony which is very profitable to mankind. And so the authentic divine dogmas and the honour of the clergy are at the head of our preoccupations.

This is a restatement of the Christian hellenist idea of the relationship between Church and State, as held from the time of Constantine the Great, except that the position of the clergy has been considerably upgraded.

In May 535 Justinian issued his Novella 9 which affirmed the honour due to the city of Old Rome, the seat of the pontificate; and in a letter to Pope John II he spoke of the Roman church as "caput omnium ecclesiarum". In another letter, to the patriarch Epiphanius, he says: "We have condemned Nestorius and Eutyches, taking care to preserve in all things the unity of the holy churches with the most holy pope and patriarch of Old Rome. . . . For we cannot tolerate that anything concerning church order should not be reported to his holiness, for he is the head of all the holy priests of God, and each time that heretics have risen among us it is by sentence and right judgement of this venerable see that they have been condemned."[12]

These imperial edicts present a very "high" doctrine of the papacy, which was accepted everywhere in the East as being in accordance with apostolic tradition. Justinian no doubt knew of Novella 27 of the Emperor Valentinian, published in July 445. It was intended to curb the pretensions of Hilary, bishop of Arles, who had been seeking to extend his jurisdiction to territories outside his diocese, without the Pope's permission. This novella says: "Because the primacy of the apostolic see has been confirmed by the merits of St Peter, the prince of the episcopal *corona*, by the dignity of the city of Rome, and also by the authority of the holy synods, let no one seek to do anything that is illicit without the authority of this see. For the peace of the churches will be finally and everywhere preserved when they are subject to their supreme ruler."[13]

The reference here to the papal authority being "confirmed" by the authority of the holy synods is of particular interest and importance. The holy synods are the general councils of the whole church. If the holy see had continued to work ordinarily within the framework of the general councils the final schism between East and West would probably not have come about. If the Bishop of Rome had been content to govern the Church synodically, seeing his primacy as something that operated within the "episcopal corona", and not as something to be imposed upon it from outside, the papacy would not be in the straits that it is in today. Also it would probably never have developed into a temporal monarchy. This serious misdevelopment was buttressed by the False Decretals and the equally spurious Donation of Constantine (8th–9th century), products of the tradition of thought in the papal curia. That these documents were fabrications was not known until the sixteenth century. There is a certain irony in the fact that St John Fisher and St Thomas More made use of them in their defence of the papacy.

By assuming temporal sovereignty, in spite of Christ's words "Regnum meum non est de hoc mundo",[14] the Pope attempted to combine in his own person the two rôles of *sacerdotium* and *imperium*, and inevitably was unable to sustain either rôle properly.

This alienated the sympathies of the East still further; and also, by the end of the seventh-century civil upheavals in the empire had already caused new breakdowns of communication between East and West. But apart from these political factors in the estrangement of the two churches, there had been a long history of tensions and suspicions between them. For instance, at the Second Council of Nicaea in 787 the Iconoclastic Controversy, over the veneration to be given to sacred images, was ended. The Council had been summoned by the Empress Irene, and Pope Hadrian I had sent two legates. The Council declared its acceptance of the doctrine set out by the Pope in a letter he had sent to the Empress and her son Constantine. This letter was read in the Council's second session.[15] In the Greek translation that was read a number of passages emphasising the Roman primacy were omitted; and wherever St Peter's name was mentioned as founder of the Roman see, St Paul's name was added. The Pope's protest, renewing a protest made previously by St Gregory the Great, against the Patriarch of Constantinople's use of the title "Ecumenical Patriarch", was also omitted.[16]

These omissions in the Greek version of the Pope's letter are significant. They show that the Easterns were conscious of what they felt to be a tendency on the part of popes to press the implications of their primacy too far; they were jealous, and rightly so, for the legitimate autonomy of their churches within the federation of local churches which together made up the Church Catholic.

Up till the fourth century St Paul's name had always been bracketed with St Peter's when the foundation of the Roman church was mentioned; the habit of dropping St Paul's name, which gradually became general, is symptomatic of the Western tendency to place a "maximalist" interpretation on everything Petrine, and this was bound to be disturbing to Easterns.

The Roman insistence on the principle of apostolicity in the organisation of the Church gradually gained ground among the Orientals and considerably influenced their thought. During the eighth and ninth centuries it became increasingly accepted in the East that the ultimate direction of religious affairs should rest with the bishops of the five patriarchal sees: Rome, Constantinople, Alexandria, Antioch, and Jerusalem, who were seen as the authentic and authoritative representatives of the *sacerdotium*, the primacy of the Roman patriarch being fully acknowledged.

The patriarchates were major areas of ecclesiastical jurisdiction. They evolved over several centuries, the patriarchs only gradually becoming distinct from metropolitans and exarchs. The patriarchates took their final form after the Council of Chalcedon (451), but were already taking shape in the fourth century, as the sixth canon of the Council of Nicaea shows. This canon said: "Let ancient custom be observed throughout Egypt, Libya, and

Pentapolis, so that the Bishop of Alexandria has authority over all these districts, as is the custom with the bishop of the city of Rome [i.e., over Western parts of the Roman empire]. Similarly with regard to Antioch and other provinces, let their privileges be observed in the churches."[17] This can be used neither as an argument for or against the Roman primacy, since a clear distinction must be made between the Pope's jurisdiction as bishop and patriarch, and the authority that belongs to his primacy. In the early centuries there was comparatively little centralisation in the Western Church. The Pope's power in the West was actually less than that of the Bishop of Alexandria in the East. He did not ordinarily intervene in local councils, nor in the appointment of bishops. The great impetus towards centralisation came with the reign of Leo the Great; it was checked by the barbarian invasions, but was resumed later.

A modern authority[18] says that "Catholic writers in the East believed the patriarchal system to be an essential element in the Church, not, however, *jure divino*, but *jure ecclesiastico*, as a result of historical evolution. Thus they held that the ordinary method of managing the affairs of the universal church pertained to an assembly of all the patriarchs, in such a way, however, as not to deny that to one of them, namely the Bishop of Rome, belonged a real authority over the others, and a true primacy."

This idea of the Pentarchy, as it was called, had appeared clearly for the first time in the legislation of Justinian, especially in his Novella 109. The Emperor's edicts, as we have seen, always gave special weight to the position and prerogatives of the see of Rome. The theory of the Pentarchy was in no way anti-papal.

The idea of the Pentarchy is explained in a letter of St Theodore of Studios (759–826), monastic reformer, to Leo the Sacellarius. He says:

> We are not talking about worldly affairs. It is the Emperor and the secular tribunal who have the right to judge in such concerns. What we are concerned with are divine and heavenly decisions; and these are reserved to no one else but those to whom the Word of God said: Whatsoever you shall bind on

earth shall be bound in heaven, and whatsoever you shall loose on earth shall be loosed also in heaven. Who are these men to whom this order has been given? The Apostles and their successors. And who are the successors of the Apostles? He who presides at Rome, and is the first; he who presides at Constantinople, and is the second; and after them those of Alexandria, Antioch, and Jerusalem. This is the pentarchic authority of the Church. It is to them that belongs the power of decision concerning the divine dogmas. The Emperor and the secular authority have the duty of assisting them and confirming their decisions.[19]

The theory of the Pentarchy was not without supporters in Rome. One of them was Anastasius the Librarian, a native of Rome who had been educated by Greek monks and who attended the final session of the eighth General Council (Constantinople IV) in the year 870. In his preface to his translation of the acts of this council he says:[20]

> As Christ has placed in his body, the Church, patriarchs to the same number as the senses of our mortal body, nothing can be lacking for the well-being of the Church when these sees are united in one will, just as nothing can be lacking in the functioning of the body when the five senses are whole and healthy. Because the see of Rome has the precedence among these sees, one may justly compare it with the sense of sight, which among all the senses is assuredly the first, being the most vigilant, and remaining, more than any other, in communion with the rest.

Since the most serious difficulty today in the way of reunion between the Catholic and Orthodox churches is the question of the Papacy, this idea of the Pentarchy is one that might well be revived. There can be no reunion without major concessions from the West, since the Easterns cannot accept any interpretation of the Roman primacy that goes beyond what was admitted, explicitly or tacitly, by the first General Councils, and what was generally accepted between the Fourth Council and the ultimate schism. It is hard to see why Rome should feel the need to ask for more than this. If the primacy as so understood were to be recognised by the East, and if then the higher direction of the reunited church were to be entrusted to the Patriarchs of the five apostolic sees, under the presidency of the Roman patriarch, this would be ample safeguard against errors of judgement on the part of the Pope, which are almost inevitable, from time to time, when he acts alone and uncollegially.[21]

The idea of the Pentarchy continued to be held in the East, but after the schism it acquired anti-Roman overtones, and it began to be claimed that the five patriarchs existed *jure divino*, and with absolute equality of power. Little more was heard of the Pentarchy after the Moscow patriarchate, which had been set up to replace the Roman, was abolished by Peter the Great. (The patriarchate of Moscow was revived only in 1917.)

Since the schism Constantinople has been regarded by the Orthodox as the senior patriarchate, but with a primacy of honour only. The general view among the Orthodox today is that the administrative basis of each autocephalous church is the synodal system, and that patriarchs are distinguished from metropolitans, and metropolitans from diocesan bishops, only on account of their precedence and certain privileges.

In the ninth century a major breakdown between Rome and Constantinople was caused by the schism of Photius, who was patriarch of Constantinople from the year 858. The whole question of Photius's excommunication and the schism is extremely complex. Since the publication in 1948 of François Dvornik's *The Photian Schism* older Western views of the schism can no longer be sustained. Certainly Photius can no longer be regarded as a bitter opponent of the Roman primacy. "On this point", Dr Dvornik says in his *Byzance et la primauté romaine*, "recent studies show that we must radically change our opinion."

The council of union of 879–880 which healed the schism called upon each side to be tolerant in the matter of different liturgical rites and customs as between East and West. Unhappily, this appeal was widely ignored by both sides. Minor matters, such as the use of leavened or unleavened bread in the eucharist, continued to be the subject of bitter polemics. The hoped-for new period of good relations between Constantinople and Rome was not achieved.

East-West relations continued uneasily until Pope Leo IX (1048–1054) attempted to extend his jurisdiction to certain Byzantine territories in southern Italy where there were both Greek and Latin churches. The Pope, relying on the False Decretals, embodying the Donation of Constantine, asserted his direct power, civil as well as ecclesiastical, over the whole of Italy, and appointed a Latin archbishop for Sicily, which had always been considered Byzantine territory. Similar tactics were employed in Apulia, another traditionally Byzantine area. More harm was done by Latin ecclesiastics in these areas attacking the Greek liturgical usages. The patriarch Michael Cerularius retaliated by threatening to close all the Latin churches in Constantinople unless they adopted the Greek rite.

The pamphlets and letters sent to Constantinople by the Cardinal Humbert of Silva Candida, who was appointed in 1054 to head a papal mission to Constantinople, showed the Greeks what they were up against. Humbert made it plain that what was intended was to extend direct and absolute papal rule over all bishops and faithful everywhere. This was rightly seen to be contrary to the Eastern traditions which had previously been accepted by Rome. The policy implied the virtual extinction of the autonomy of the Eastern churches within the one catholic unity, and their eventual Latinisation. Humbert complained in his *Opus Tripartitum* that the Greeks "do not understand what is said to them with reasons, but always adhere to some councils or other, and to what has been handed on to them by their predecessors".[22]

When the papal mission arrived in Constantinople the Pope was dead. Humbert and the other legates knew this, and that because of the Pope's death their commission had expired. Notwithstanding, the Cardinal excommunicated the Patriarch, and after placing the letter of excommunication on the altar of the church of St Sophia he left the city. The bull accused the Easterns of various heresies, charged them with simony—then rampant in the West—

condemned their married clergy, and accused them of having suppressed the *Filioque* clause in the Creed. The clause was in fact a Latin innovation, and had been introduced in contravention of the decrees of the Council of Nicaea. Christ had taught that the Holy Ghost was sent by God the Father; the Creed was amended so that it was affirmed that the Third Person of the Trinity "proceeded" from the Father *and the Son* (*Filioque*).

The Emperor convoked a synod, which condemned the bull. A copy of it was burned, and Humbert and the other legates were excommunicated.

The Patriarch Cerularius did not denounce either the Pope or the Latin Church; the legates only were excommunicated. On the Eastern side there was no formal rejection of the Roman primacy, and no schism was created; but the effect was much the same.

Negotiations were opened under Pope Victor II, and again under his successors Stephen IX and Alexander II. The reforming cardinal St Peter Damian (1007–1072) addressed a letter to the patriarch "Against the Errors of the Greeks concerning the 'procession' of the Holy Ghost". In spite of this unconciliatory title, Damian's chapter "On the authority of the Roman Pontiff" seems to have been found basically acceptable. The opening sentences of his letter are of interest for more than one reason.

Greatly to be praised [says the writer] is the prudence of your holiness . . . which, for the solution of the question of the Holy Spirit, addresses itself not to anyone, but especially to Peter, whom your holiness undoubtedly knows has received the keys of authority and of holy wisdom. . . . Blessed art thou, Simon Bar-Jona, Christ says, because flesh and blood have not revealed it to thee, but my Father who is in heaven. For the Creator of the world chose this man, from among all other mortals on earth, and to him he granted to hold in the Church by right of perpetual privilege the chair of teaching authority. So that anyone who wishes to know anything pertaining to the divine mysteries (*divinum aliquid et profundum*) must recur to the oracular power and doctrine of this teacher (*ad hujus praeceptoris oraculum doctrinamque recurrit*).[23]

However one may translate the phrase *hujus praeceptoris oraculum*, it can only be seen as a relatively early example of that "oracular" conception of the papal office which, in spite of the measures taken to exclude it at Vatican I in 1870, has never ceased to flourish among Roman Catholics, and seems even to have affected the thought of some of the popes themselves, not least since 1870.

St Peter Damian's overtures to the Greeks came to nothing; but they showed that even after 1054 discussion between the two churches was still possible.

During the eleventh century the Byzantine empire came under threat from the Turks. The Emperor Michael VII endeavoured to obtain help from the Pope, Gregory VII (1073–1085), who was sympathetic. But Gregory's appeal to Princes—addressed actually to the Western emperor Henry IV—fell flat. The Pope had become involved in a violent conflict with Henry over the new and unbalanced papal ideology of the superiority of the spiritual power over the temporal.

Pope Gregory VII (Hildebrand) is often regarded as the supreme exponent of papal theocracy, and not without reason.[24] In his *Dictatus Papae* and other writings he virtually identifies the Roman Pontiff with Peter, and extols his primacy to the skies in language that no Eastern Christian could possibly accept. Everything, or nearly everything, is deduced from the single text "Thou art Peter" of Matthew xvi. The Pope is "the only person who may be called by right universal"—which is exactly what Gregory's predecessor St Gregory the Great had said the Pope must *not* be called—and "whose feet all princes must kiss", "whom no man may judge", who, once ordained according to canonical law, becomes indubitably holy (*indubiter sanctus*) by the merits of St Peter"; whose name is "unique in the world" and "the only one to be pronounced in all churches". The Pope's power in the Church is universal and absolute; the secular world is subject to him, so that he has authority to depose kings and emperors and "to release subjects from their duties to the wicked".

To us today this sounds like the language of delirium. We may reasonably ask where in all this is there any trace of the example set by Christ, for the instruction of St Peter, when he washed the feet of his disciples and told them that theirs was to be a ministry of service?

Yet it should be remembered that Gregory VII was by no means the sole architect of the system of medieval papalism. The hierocratic re-ordering of Christian society was an important part of the Gregorian programme, but there is a long tradition of hierocratic thought behind Gregory. The *Dictatus Papae* seem never to have been published, but are entered in the papal register under the year 1075. It is now generally recognised that they were intended as chapter headings for a new collection of canon law. They draw heavily on earlier material, such as the *Collection of 74 Titles* (Leo IX), and on the Pseudo-Isadore. Dr Walter Ullmann has emphasised in his *The Growth of Papal Government in the Middle Ages* that "Perhaps the most characteristic feature of the papal hierocratic theme had always been its conservatism and reliance on tradition" (p. 177). For instance, the claim to depose unsatisfactory emperors is implicit in the whole papal theory of the empire as apparent in the forged Donation of Constantine. The forgers, as Dr Ullmann says, did not invent the ideology which their forgeries supported. The forgeries themselves originated quite independently of the papacy, which cannot be blamed for using them.

A disastrous effect of the separation between East and West was that these extreme hierocratic ideas went virtually unchallenged. To quote Ullmann again:[25] "This papal power transcending everything on earth and responsible to nobody, was vested in a man not inappropriately styled 'admirabilis' . . . the Pope was not a mere vicar of Christ or of St Peter, but a true vicar of God on earth. For it was he who 'vices Dei gerit in terris'." Resting on his power, "the Pope was to be beyond the reach of any mortal. The idea of a papal responsibility was unanimously rejected. There was nobody on earth who could say to the Pope: 'Cur ita facies?' . . . The Pope could do and say whatever he pleased to do and say, in all and everything. 'In omnibus et per omnia potest facere et dicere quicquid placet.' . . . 'The Pope can do whatever God can do'; 'papa potest facere quicquid Deus potest.' " (The quotations here cited are from the Commentaries of Panormitanus on the Decretals.) The canonist Tancred bluntly stated that "Whatever is done by the authority of the lord Pope is done by the authority of God."

Yet Panormitanus and the Decretalists ought not to be quoted simply as if they were elaborating the position of Gregory VII. The theory and practice of papal government were not achieved all at once; there was a continued process of steady development after Gregory. The influence of Alexander III and Innocent III was just as important in developing the idea that the Pope was every man's judge-ordinary, and the source of all jurisdiction in the Church.

The Hildebrandine (as we may conveniently call it) conception of the Pope as "Lord of All" led on quite naturally to Boniface VIII's bull "Unam Sanctam" of 1302, which affirmed that all Christians are subject to Christ's vicar, the successor of St Peter, so that "if the Greeks and others say that they are not committed to Peter and his successors, they necessarily confess that they are not of Christ's sheep." The bull reaffirms also the doctrine of "the two swords"; viz., that the Church possesses both spiritual *and* temporal power, the former to be used by the clergy, the latter by princes and other civil authorities *on behalf of* the Church. "Furthermore," it says, "we declare, state, define and pronounce that it is altogether necessary to salvation for every human creature to be subject to the Roman Pontiff."

In advancing the traditional arguments, such as the allegory of the two swords (first used in the eleventh century) for the superiority of the priestly power over the civil power, the bull "Unam Sanctam" appears to make the temporal power of the papacy an article of faith.

The same spirit and doctrine were behind Pius V's bull of February 25th 1570, "Regnans in excelsis", which excommunicated the English queen Elizabeth I, and thereby involved the Pope's English adherents in a hundred years and more of bloody persecution. The bull opens with these words:

He who reigns in heaven, to whom is given all power in heaven and on earth, gave the one, holy, catholic, and apostolic church, outside of which there is no salvation, to be governed in the fullness of authority, to one man only, that is to say, to Peter, the Prince of the Apostles, and to his successor the Roman Pontiff. This one ruler he established as prince over all nations and kingdoms, to root up, destroy, dissipate, scatter, plant, and build, so that the Holy Spirit might bind together a faithful people, united in the bond of mutual charity, and present it safe and sound to the Saviour.

By this time the primacy had come a long way indeed, and was hardly to be recognised any more as having anything to do with the solemn words addressed by Christ to the Fisherman on the shore of the sea of Galilee.

A modern historian[26] has ample grounds for his conviction that from the principles of Gregory VII and the canonists are directly descended the doctrines of papal infallibility[27] and the absolute necessity of membership of the Roman Church for salvation.[28]

To return now to the eleventh century: in 1089 renewed overtures were made to Constantinople by Pope Urban II. The emperor Henry IV acted as intermediary, but the efforts were again fruitless; partly because the Pope was still claiming direct rights over the Byzantine areas of southern Italy. The Easterns on their side were still denouncing the "errors" of the Latins, notably the *Filioque* clause in the Creed and the use of unleavened bread in the Mass. Some Easterns, however, exercised moderation in the controversy. Theophylact, archbishop of Ochrida, declared that differences of rite and custom were not so important as to justify a state of schism, and ought to be considered in a spirit of charity. He remarked, pointedly, that although intransigent Latins might think to honour Peter and his power of the keys, they dishonoured him if they destroyed what he had built up, and broke up the foundations of the Church that he was supposed to uphold.[29] For Theophylact, the *Filioque* was a greater obstacle to union than the primacy.

In 1095 the Emperor Alexis I made a new appeal to the West for help in repelling the Turks. In response the Pope called for volunteers to help free the Holy Places in Jerusalem. Antioch was reconquered and its Greek patriarch reinstalled. Previously, cordial relations had been established between the papal legate and the patriarch of Jerusalem.

In 1098 at the Synod of Bari the Pope discussed reunion with the Greeks of Italy and Byzantium. But the Pope's death put an end to the project for a further synod at Rome in the year following, and relations deteriorated when the crusade's leader, Bohemond, announced that he was going to retain Antioch as a fief for himself and his family.

In 1100 a Latin patriarch was installed at Antioch, and from then on the Greek patriarch resided at Constantinople. The population and the undisciplined crusading army remained on bad terms because of the looting and robbery that went on. The Greeks, not without justification, began to look on the Latins as barbarians; the Latins blamed the Greeks, whose advice they despised and ignored, for the disasters they encountered.

In 1136 a debate took place in Constantinople between Anselm of Havelberg (a Latin) and Nicetas, bishop of Nicomedia. Anselm took a high line in explaining the papal primacy, and was tactless enough to represent the papacy as a faultless centre of unity, and the church of Constantinople, by contrast, as a nursery of all the heresies. In so far as the Early Church heresies were mostly hatched in the East, there was something in what Anselm said; but he could have made his point more effectively without such exaggeration. It was made again eight hundred years later by Monsignor Duchesne, who says in his *Eglises séparées* that the Seven Ecumenical Councils belong as much to the West as to the East, although they were held in the East and were convoked by the Emperor. "But for the most part they only represent an orthodox Roman victory over an Eastern heresy; or, to speak more charitably, a remedy applied by the Latin Church to her Greek sister infected by some doctrinal malady."

The Russian philosopher and theologian Vladimir Soloviev (1853–1900), a worker for Christian unity who eventually joined the Catholic Church, but without abandoning his critical attitude towards the Latins, declared that Duchesne was right. "Arius",

Soloviev says,[30] "was an Eastern. Eusebius of Nicomedia, his great sympathiser, was an Eastern. The Council of Nicaea found its chief supporters in the West. . . . Macedonius and Apollinaris, condemned at Constantinople, again were Easterns. . . . It is a patriarch of Constantinople who is condemned at Ephesus, and two more Easterns are anathematised at Chalcedon. And from the West comes the outstanding document of the faith of Chalcedon— the Tome of Leo. . . . If there is one place in the world more than another where they can claim the Seven Ecumenical Councils it is Rome; . . . and if there is one place more than another where the mention of them can raise gloomy reflections, it ought to be in Constantinople."

All the same, after hearing Anselm of Havelberg's "oracular" idea of the papal office, Nicetas was entitled to ask as he did: if the authority of the Pope is really of this nature, of what use are Scripture, sacred studies, and Greek wisdom? If it really is so, then by all means let the Pope remain the sole bishop and master. "But, if he wishes to have fellow-workers in the Lord's vineyard, let him remain in the humility of his primacy, and not ill-treat his brethren. The truth of Christ has brought us to birth in the womb of the Church not for servitude but for freedom."[31]

Towards the end of the twelfth century the Emperors continued to cultivate good relations with the Papacy; but by now the Hildebrandine church-state ideology had become an insuperable barrier to any rapprochement. The approaches made by the Emperor towards reunion were resented by the Eastern clergy and faithful after their experience of the Crusaders. In 1182 the infuriated Greeks had massacred the Latin residents of Constantinople, and the West reacted with the conviction that the only remedy was to conquer Constantinople and replace the Greek emperor with a Latin one.

In 1204 this was achieved by the Fourth Crusade, in circumstances of the maximum horror. Franks and Flemings indulged in an orgy of vandalism, rape, and destruction, and the city was reduced to a shambles.

After the conquest the patriarchs were appointed by papal nomination, and bishops also, without imperial confirmation—a state of affairs which continued until the Greeks recovered the city in 1261. Such things were unheard of in the East, and the Greeks were reduced to despair. The anonymous author of a short treatise entitled *Why have the Latins oppressed us?* wrote bitterly about the spoliation of churches, the extrusion of the Greek clergy, for whom Latin clerks were substituted, and the appointment of a Venetian, Thomas Morosini, as patriarch. The outraged author denies absolutely the doctrine of the papal primacy, and even the primacy of St Peter. Thenceforward Greek theologians tended to be entirely negative in their attitude to the question of the primacy. There was no lessening of their traditional reverence for the apostle Peter, and the decrees of the early councils remained unchallenged, as did the decrees of the emperors affirming Rome's first place in the hierarchy.

After 1204 all possibility of union between East and West was virtually at an end, though even now efforts to reach a settlement continued to be made. Formulas of union were signed at the Second Council of Lyons (1274) and at the Council of Florence (1445), but the only validity that these settlements had was on paper. The reunions of 1274 and 1445 were made on the Emperor's initiative and under political duress. In 1274 the Greeks hoped to use the Pope to stave off the attack of Charles of Anjou; in 1445 they wanted Eastern help against the Turks. The mass of the people in Constantinople remained hostile to the idea of unity, and members of the Greek clergy who favoured union found themselves boycotted. After Florence, the Emperor delayed over promulgation of the decree of union. This was taken to mean that he thought unfavourably of it, and so the people were confirmed in their intransigence. Most of the Easterns who had signed the decree at Florence seem afterwards to have regretted doing so.

During the thirteenth century some Western Decretists and canonists, most notably Huguccio, took a low view of papal prerogatives *vis-à-vis* the authority of general councils; but these views represent only one strain in canonistic speculation about the primacy. The general opinion of the thirteenth-century Decretalists is overwhelmingly papalist.

Some, however, who were thinking along these newer lines believed that they had found support for their view in the twelfth-century work known as the *Decretum Gratiani*, a collection of patristic texts, conciliar decrees, and papal pronouncements assembled by Gratian, the "father of canon law". As might be expected of a vast compilation of this kind, texts could be found in it favouring both a "high" and a "low" view of papal authority. The Decretists, as they came to be called, concentrated on the latter. From their studies in the *Decretum* they developed a theory of church authority, which they believed to correspond to the ecclesiastical polity of the Early Church.

"In Decretist thought", says its most recent historian,[32] "there were at least two institutions through which the inherent authority of the whole church could be expressed, the Papacy and the General Council; and in questions of faith, and other matters which affected the well-being of the whole church, the authority of the Council was to be preferred to that of the Pope."

The Decretists held that the Church as such was preserved by virtue of Christ's promises from believing or teaching erroneously, but that this indefectibility applied to the *whole* church, and not to any particular individual in it, such as the Pope. The Pope and the General Council represented the supreme teaching authority of the Church; and of these the authority of the Council was the greater.

When they said that the Pope was bound by the Council, or that in matters of doctrine the Council was greater than the Pope, the Decretists seem to have meant that when the Pope issued decrees together with the Fathers of the Council, such decrees possessed a higher authority than those issued by the Pope alone. As Tierney says: "For them, it was of the essence of a General Council that the Pope or his legate should preside over it."

What the Decretists were looking for was some means of imposing a constitutional limitation on the Pope's powers. Huguccio, Bishop of Pisa, who was the author of a *Summa* on the *Decretum*, held that when it was said that the Roman church had never erred in matters of faith, what was meant was the *whole* Catholic Church in communion with the Roman bishop; or at the very least the whole local Roman church, in the sense that even if the Pope himself erred, the entire body of Roman cardinals, clergy, and faithful would not do so.

These and similar speculations were re-presented, in sharper terms and more orderly form, by the later Conciliarists: those who maintained without equivocation that the ultimate and supreme source of ecclesiastical authority is the universal church, clergy and faithful together.

Dom Paul de Vooght summarises Conciliarist thought in this way:[33]

> In the thought of the Conciliarists the Pope is a constitutional monarch. He is the supreme organ of the Church's executive; but he is capable of correction. He is subordinate, in principle, to the legislative and judiciary powers exercised by the General Council.
>
> If the Pope fails in his duty, the Council can judge him, depose him, and install another in his place. It is true that normally the convening of the Council belongs to the Pope; but in case of necessity it can be summoned by others, and even against the Pope's will. In every respect the general principles which apply to every government and to every law are applicable to the Pope and his governing authority. Governments and laws are legitimate and binding in conscience only in so far as they correspond to their end. In the Church this end can be nothing other than charity. From the moment when the Pope goes against charity he is blameworthy and answerable to the Council. The Pope presides over the Church's destinies *ad aedificationem*, not *ad destructionem*!

The development of this line of thought received considerable impetus during the Great Schism which split the Latin Church itself in the fourteenth and fifteen centuries. On April 8th 1378 Bartholomew Prignani, Archbishop of Bari, was elected Pope and took the name Urban VI. Four months later the cardinals declared the election invalid because of duress. They declared the Holy See vacant, and elected a new pope, Clement VII (Robert of Geneva), who ranks as an anti-pope and must not be confused with the

Clement who was elected in 1523. Urban refused to accept his deposition, and maintained his court in Rome. Clement established himself at Avignon. The Western church was divided, some sovereigns and princes supporting Urban, others Clement. Religious orders pledged their loyalties differently, or were themselves divided. The struggle between the two claimants to the papal throne became a constitutional crisis in which the basic issue was whether or not the Pope should continue to govern the Church in the undiluted absolutist and old monarchic manner, or whether the cardinals in curia should participate in acts of papal sovereignty, as had been the custom in the thirteenth and fourteenth centuries. This was a natural time for the revival of theories which emphasised the authority of the *whole* church.

In discussing these questions it must have seemed evident to many that in the last resort it had to be *the General Council* that possessed the supreme authority; for, unless one of two or more papal claimants should give way and resign, what other way was there of resolving the problem and identifying a lawful pope?

It is not inconceivable that such a situation may one day occur again. In fact, there is a rival pope at the present time, Clement XV, who has his seat in France, and was expelled from Italy by the civil authorities in February 1969 while on his way to pray at the tomb of his "predecessor" John XXIII. So far, however, Pope Clement has attracted no great following, and seems unlikely to do so in spite of his programme, which includes the correction of the "errors" of Paul VI.

The Great Schism dragged on, with disastrous consequences, until in 1417 there were three claimants to the papal throne. In 1409 the Council of Pisa, which had been convoked by the cardinals and claimed to be ecumenical,[34] had deposed the rival claimants, Benedict XIII and Gregory XII, and elected the cardinal Peter Philargi, who took the name of Alexander V. But this did not end the schism since Gregory and Benedict refused to recognise the Council. It is still a matter of dispute whether Alexander V can be admitted to be in the true line of papal succession or not.

Eventually the schism was ended by the Council of Constance

(1414–18), which is recognised by Catholics as ecumenical since it was summoned by Pope John XXIII the First. This seems on the face of it illogical. Since Angelo Roncalli assumed the name of John XXIII in 1958 the presumption would appear to be that the first John XXIII (Baldassare Cossa) was no true pope. If so, no council of his convening could be ecumenical, if one grants the assumption that a General Council *must* be convened by the Pope. But as we have seen, this view was not held in the primitive church.

The Council of Constance demanded the abdication of all three claimants, John XXIII, Gregory XII, and Benedict XIII. In 1415 John fled; he was recaptured and brought back to the Council, which then deposed him and elected as the new pope Otto Colonna, who took the name Martin V. This election was acknowledged by the whole Latin church.

The Council continued, and in its fifth session passed the canon known as *Sacrosancta*,[35] which said:

> This holy synod of Constance . . . declares that being legitimately assembled in the Holy Ghost, constituting a General Council and representing the catholic church, it derives its authority directly from Christ; and to it everyone, of whatever rank and dignity, including the Pope, is subject in matters which belong to the faith, the ending of the schism, and the reform of the church in its head and members.

In 1417 the Council passed the decree *Frequens*, which stipulated that general councils were in future to be held frequently. The next was to be held in five years' time, the one following seven years later; after that, they were to be held regularly every ten years. These intervals might be shortened, but not lengthened.

However, Martin V, once he was secure on the throne, asserted that councils were subordinate to the Pope, and that reforms must be left to him.

Eventually Martin convoked a General Council at Basel, in 1431. But he died in the same year, and his successor, Eugenius IV, dissolved the Council on account of unfavourable reports. The Council refused to accept the decree of dissolution, and reaffirmed the decrees of Constance which proclaimed the Council's superiority over the Pope. Then, under pressure from the Emperor, Eugenius revoked his suppression of the Council, and recognised it. The Council then took a strongly conciliarist line, imposing certain restrictions on the papal legates and prescribing an oath to be taken by the Pope after his election.

In 1436 Eugenius circulated to Catholic princes a memorandum denouncing the Council's "usurpations". He transferred the Council to Ferrara, as a more convenient meeting place for the Greek envoys whom he was expecting; but a proportion of the conciliar Fathers objected to this and continued in session at Basel, deposing the Pope as a heretic, and electing a new one Felix V.

Felix V is of particular interest in that he was a layman when elected. He was then Amadeo VIII, Duke of Savoy. Amadeo was a widower who now lived a celibate and religious life as dean of the Knights of St Maurice, a religious order which he had founded. He was elected after five ballots, and after much discussion. Some of the electors said that to elect a layman and a secular prince would seem to lower the credit of the ecclesiastical body, as it would look as if the clergy could provide no one worthy of the office. Others thought that a man who had been married, and who had several children, was not suitable. It was also said that the Bishop of Rome ought to be a doctor of divinity and pre-eminent in sacred learning.

Amadeo's supporters replied that he had sufficient learning, and that although not a cleric he was perfectly familiar with the breviary. He was the founder of a monastery, and also an exemplary ruler, which was what the Church needed. He was a man of ascetical life; and as to his being a widower, St Peter and others of the Apostles had been married. There was, in fact, no objection to the election even of a man whose wife was still living. The only problem would be what to do with her.

Aeneas Sylvius Piccolomini (later Pope Pius II), who was present at the Council, records in his *Commentaries* a long and eloquent speech which he made in favour of Amadeo. He ended by saying: "Come now, I beg of you to elect him for the sake of the virtuous. He will increase faith, correct morals, maintain the authority of the Church, restrain its enemies, and give peace to the Christian people. Have you not heard that those who foretell the future, when prophesying these upheavals of the Church, fixed for them this fortieth year which is now upon us as the end of the tribulation? Surely for a long time you have been hearing that a pope should be chosen at this time who would comfort Sion and set all things in peace? Who, I beseech you, will he be who can fulfill such things unless we take this man?"[36]

The election of Felix, however, reduced the Council's prestige. Its numbers fell off, and in 1438 the rump-council was expelled from Basel to Lausanne, where it submitted to the new Roman pope, Nicholas V, successor to Eugenius IV, who had remained unaffected by his deposition by the Council. Felix abdicated after a brief pontificate of two years. His cardinals retained their dignity; Felix himself became a cardinal, and Bishop of Geneva, as well as papal legate for life in Savoy. He received a pension, and was allowed to continue to wear the papal vesture and insignia, and to be addressed as "Holy Father".

Those who had voted at Basel for the deposition of Eugenius IV did so largely on the grounds that by dissolving the Council, as he had at first done, Eugenius had attempted, what was impossible and *ultra vires* for the Pope, to dissolve a General Council against its will.

That part of the Council which had assembled at Ferrara in 1438 was transferred to Florence on account of the plague, where it reopened in January 1439. The object of the Council was now to heal the schism between East and West. Eugenius was determined also to use the Council as an opportunity to reassert the rights of the Holy See on Hildebrandine lines, and to put an end to conciliarism. Father Joseph Gill, the historian of the Council of Florence, says that Eugenius's "chief claim to fame in the Church is perhaps ... his indomitable courage in withstanding the Conciliarists and safeguarding the traditional constitution of the Church."[37] That is certainly one way of looking at it; but it must be remembered that this "tradition" was not primitive, and had never been accepted by the Eastern Church. Both

Decretists and Conciliarists had appealed to earlier, and largely forgotten, ideas of church order, for whose validity a strong case could be made.

On paper, the reunion negotiations at Florence were successful; in practice, they were of no effect. The Greeks accepted the Double Procession of the Holy Ghost (the *Filioque* doctrine), and also the papal primacy as expressed in these words of the bull *Laetentur caeli*, which was signed on July 5th 1439:

> Also in the same way we define that the holy apostolic See and the Roman Pontiff hold the primacy over the whole world, and that the Roman Pontiff himself is the successor of blessed Peter, prince of the apostles, and that he is the true Vicar of Christ, head of the whole Church, and father and teacher of all Christians, and that to him in blessed Peter was given plenary power of feeding, ruling, and governing the whole Church, as contained also in the Acts of the oecumenical councils and the sacred canons."

The decree reaffirmed the order of precedence of the patriarchates as given in the ancient canons: Rome, Constantinople, Alexandria, Antioch, and Jerusalem.

When the Greeks had departed, the constitution *Etsi non dubitemus* was passed affirming the superiority of the Pope over the Council.

After the Council of Florence a high or ultramontane doctrine of the papal supremacy remained dominant in the Latin Church until very recently. The decrees of the Second Vatican Council have moderated it slightly through their emphasis on episcopal collegiality; but it was not until the publication of Paul VI's encyclical "Humanae Vitae" that Catholics became clearly aware that the theology of the papacy which had held the field for so long was in drastic need of revision.

The Fifth Lateran Council (1512–17) condemned the decrees of the Council of Pisa. The Council of Trent (1545–63) had nothing special to say about the Pope, but it rejected the request of the Protestants who attended its twenty-fourth session that it should define the supremacy of the General Council over the Pope.

During the classical age of the canonists—the twelfth to fourteenth centuries—some of the leading exponents of conciliarist or near-conciliarist ideas were Frenchmen. Outstanding among them were Jean Gerson and his friend Pierre d'Ailly, whom Gerson succeeded as chancellor of the university of Paris. The tradition remained alive in the French church, and later became known as Gallicanism: a body of thought which aimed in various ways at minimising the papal authority over bishops and national churches. The Four Gallican Articles, drawn up by the great Bossuet, and published in 1682, denied that the Pope had dominion over things temporal, and upheld the decrees of the Council of Constance, which placed the authority of General Councils above that of the Pope. The fourth article asserted that between General Councils judgements of the Pope were not irreformable. Similar ideas were held by some of the clergy in other countries.

In 1870, at the First Vatican Council, the monarchic doctrine of the papacy was given new strength by the promulgation of the doctrine of papal Infallibility, an event that was hailed by most Catholics at the time as a triumph, but which has since turned out to be a considerable liability.

"Infallibility", as the decree of 1870 makes clear, is a charism which Christ has bestowed on his Church. What is basically meant by the term is that those interpretations of revealed doctrine to which the consensus of the Church has been given will correctly mediate the original "deposit" of the faith, and so cannot mislead.

Christ gave his Apostles authority to teach in his name: "All authority has been given unto me in heaven and on earth. Go ye therefore, and make disciples of all the nations, baptising them into the name of the Father, and of the Son, and of the Holy Ghost: teaching them to observe all things whatsoever I have commanded you: and lo, I am with you always, even unto the end of the world" (Matthew xxviii, 18–20). This commission was to last until the end of time, and so passed from the Apostles to those who came after them; in teaching, they would have the assistance of the Holy Ghost. "He that heareth you, heareth me."

The words "infallible" and "infallibility" are, of course, not to be found in the New Testament writings; but the idea of an indefectible teaching authority may be found there. Thus, the Apostles and others at the very first council of all, at Jerusalem, prefaced their decisions with the words "It has seemed good to the Holy Ghost and to us. . . ." (Acts xv, 28). In her explanation of the truths committed to her by her Founder the Church uses the best words she can, both to clarify their meaning and to remove heterodox interpretations; but what are the best words today may not be the best words tomorrow. To give an example, the word "Person", taken over from current Greek philosophy, was in the fourth century an excellent tool with which to elucidate the doctrine of the Holy Trinity. It is still a word which the theologian cannot dispense with, but it is much less effective today, although nothing has been found to replace it, because our understanding of the words "person" and "persons" is different from that of the ancient Greeks. Similarly with the use of the terms "substance" and "accidents", taken over by the medieval Scholastics from the philosophy of Aristotle, to guide the thought of believers correctly in the matter of the holy eucharist: these two words are now probably incapable of conveying to most of us any intelligible meaning at all.

In 1870 the Fathers of Vatican I decided that the words which they needed to qualify the nature of the Church's teaching authority were "infallible" and "infallibility". These words have not worn well, especially as applied to the rôle of the Pope as one of the organs by which the teaching of the Church is made known. Their use has in fact meant, in spite of formal definitions which exclude this concept, that the Pope has been, and is, widely regarded by Catholics as a kind of oracle. This way of thinking goes back, as we have seen, a very long way, and seems endemic in the Latin Church in spite of all the careful formulations of its theologians.

"Infallibility" is neither a matter of revelation nor of inspiration. The formulas of Vatican I exclude these concepts from the notion of infallibility, which is seen as a purely *negative* charism whereby the Holy Spirit prevents the Church from committing herself formally to anything that is contrary to the mind of her

Founder with respect to the truths which he has entrusted to her for the salvation of mankind.

The present Pope, on the other hand—like some of his predecessors—has at times used language which seems to indicate an oracular or inspirational view of his office. Speaking at Bogotá on August 25th 1968, and referring to theologians who had criticised aspects of his encyclical "Humanae Vitae", the Pope said:

> Today some have recourse to ambiguous doctrinal expressions and others arrogate to themselves the permission to proclaim their own personal opinions, on which they confer that authority which they, more or less covertly, question in him who by divine right possesses such a protected and awesome charism."

Again, at his general audience on March 24th 1969 the Pope suggested that the Holy Spirit gives his inspiration "by preference" to the Pope above other members of the Church. The inspirations of the Holy Spirit, he said, were given to the ecclesial community to build the Church, and "by preference to the one who has a special directive function" within it.

Most of the Catholic faithful, who have never read the decree "Pastor Aeternus" of Vatican I defining the Pope's infallibility, take an oracular and inspirational view of the Pope's function. Thus a correspondent writing in *The Tablet* of September 14th 1968, and arguing, paradoxically, that the case against contraception is more apparent now than it was in the days of Pius XI, ended his letter by saying: "I believe that God has told the Holy Father this, giving him an earlier warning than he has given to some of us." The writer was an educated man, with some reputation as a Catholic author and publicist.

If literate and sophisticated Catholics confuse papal infallibility with inspiration, it is not to be wondered at that numbers of the "simple faithful" do so.

In the triumphalist days of Pio Nono the word "infallibility" obviously had a great appeal; it should be realised by now that it is a dangerous and unsatisfactory tool, unsuitable for the work for which it was designed.

It is significant that among the "Exceptiones", or objections, put forward to the wording of the Infallibility decree when it was being prepared in 1870 was the suggestion that for the words "infallible" and "infallibility" there should be substituted the words "free from error" or "immune from error".[38] It seems a pity that the suggestion was not accepted.

The Eastern Church holds the doctrinal definitions of General Councils—and they acknowledge that to be binding such decrees should be signed by the first bishop, the bishop of Rome—to be inerrant. The Latin Church holds the same belief, but has declared also that under certain conditions the decrees of popes acting alone, apart from any Council, are inerrant; and further, that such papal definitions are binding of themselves, apart from any subsequent consent of the Church. The two viewpoints, Eastern and Western, are irreconcilable.

Section iv of the First Dogmatic Constitution ("Pastor Aeternus") on the Church of Christ, promulgated by the First Vatican Council on July 13th 1870, says:

> Therefore . . . with the approval of the Sacred Council, We teach and define that it is a dogma divinely revealed: that the Roman Pontiff, when he speaks *ex cathedra*, that is, when in discharge of the office of Pastor and teacher of all Christians, by virtue of his supreme Apostolic authority, he defines a doctrine regarding faith or morals to be held by the universal church, is, by the divine assistance promised to him in blessed Peter, possessed of that infallibility with which the divine Redeemer willed that his Church should be endowed in defining doctrine regarding faith or morals; and that, therefore, such definitions of the Roman Pontiff are of themselves, and not from the consent of the Church, irreformable.[39]

It is well known that some of the chief proponents of the dogma, among them Cardinal Manning, were disappointed at the careful and limiting terms in which it was defined. The boisterous and extravagant W. G. ("Ideal") Ward, ex-clergyman and lay professor of divinity, an open adherent of the "oracular" idea of infallibility, said that he would like to read an *ex cathedra* papal pronouncement in his newspaper every morning. In a pastoral letter to his flock, written immediately after the Council, Manning declared that the word "define" in the decree was to be taken in a large sense, so as to include all dogmatic judgements of the Pope, including judgements on "the orthodoxy or heterodoxy of un-inspired books, legislative or judicial acts, adjudgements, sentences, or decisions which contain the motives of such acts as derive from faith or morals."

Such sentiments were in the air; so it is not surprising that Lord Acton, writing to his friend Richard Simpson on June 9th 1861, should have said: "Only a Jansenist can say that a pope or a saint was not liable to sin or error, or that the church has the same infallibility in government as in faith."[40]

In January 1870 four "Postulata contra Definitionem"—objections to the dogma as proposed—were lodged with the presidents of the Council.[41] They were signed by 136 bishops. One of the four documents was from a group of American, Irish, and English bishops, among them the Right Reverend and Honourable William Clifford, bishop of Clifton. It contained the following proposition:

> The supreme spiritual power in the Church is essentially complex and composite, so that it does not reside in Peter and his successors, but in the body of the chief pastors of the Church, that is, in the Pope and the bishops in communion with him.

A French bishop added the comment: "Si le Seigneur avait voulu attribuer à Pierre et à ses successeurs cette monarchie, aurait-il attribué une partie des pouvoirs souverains aux apôtres et à leurs successeurs?"

A proposition in another "Postulatum" said:

> The bishops gathered together in an Ecumenical Council possess in those things which pertain to faith, the extirpation of schism, and the reformation of the Church, a proper and independent right of examining, judging, accepting or rejecting the Decrees of the Roman Pontiff, even against the Pontiff's will, and of correcting him and obliging him, under pain of

deposition, to approve and promulgate the judgement of the major part of the Council.

This, of course, was pure Conciliarism. It may have been drafted by the French bishop, Moret, who had argued in public session that the powers of a Council are superior to those of a Pope.

Of the Constitution "Pastor Aeternus" Archbishop Mathew has remarked that "It may seem strange that so many bishops approved a tendency which seemed neglectful of their own rights; but they could not foresee that the impending Council would be interrupted before the rights of the episcopate could be discussed."

The Council was prematurely closed, or rather suspended, on October 20th 1870, after the occupation of Rome by Italian troops. In protest the Pope, Pio Nono, assumed his new rôle of "Prisoner of the Vatican".

Sixty-one bishops who dissented from the infallibility decree left the Council early rather than cast a negative vote in the face of the Pontiff. The genial Pope, who had celebrated his election in 1846 by inviting the cardinals to an alfresco supper on the roof of St Peter's, was much esteemed, and the passing of the definition was in some degree an expression of the bishops' sympathy with him in his troubles. All the dissenting bishops afterwards signified their adhesion to the decrees of the Council, and there was no schism.

Cardinal Manning's reaction to the passing of the decree for which he had worked so hard, and in a manner not at all points edifying, was, as we have seen, to issue a pastoral letter saying that the decree was to be interpreted in the widest possible sense. The Secretary of the Council, Monsignor Fessler, bishop of St Polten, in Austria, soon afterwards published a small book on the true meaning of the infallibility decree. Pius IX himself read and approved the treatise, and had it translated into Italian. A French edition soon followed, and in 1875 an English one.[42]

Fessler's interpretation of the dogma, which had the Pope's approval, was very different from that put forward by Ward, Manning, Louis Veuillot, and other Ultramontanes. He explains in his book that the Pope "has, however, the gift of infallibility, according to the manifest sense of the words of the definition, only as *supreme teacher of truths necessary for salvation revealed by God*." How much trouble would have been spared the Church if this had been generally received and understood. (For instance, it is obvious that the morality of birth control forms no part of Christian revelation.)

This interpretation of the infallibility decree now has the authoritative confirmation of Vatican II.

Newman had been opposed to the definition of the doctrine on the grounds that it would be "inopportune"; that is, that it would be likely to be misunderstood and misinterpreted, especially by non-Catholics. But he believed the doctrine to be true, and gave immediate acceptance to it. Three relevant passages from Newman's letters are cited by Father C. S. Dessain in his essay on "What Newman Taught in Manning's Church".[43]

The first is from a letter from Newman to the convert clergyman William Nevins written on June 19th 1864.

> As I understand the subject [Newman says] the doctrine of the Church's infallibility is primarily an inference, grounded on the Church's office of *teaching*. How could the Church be the organ of revelation and teach gospel truth without a security given to it that it should be preserved from *error* in its teaching? that is, without infallibility *so far*, infallibility in its guardianship and transmission of what the Apostles preached? The Church is the *columna et firmamentum veritatis*—Now, is this possible, unless it is guarded from going wrong, kept straight in all its formal utterances?

Writing again to the same correspondent on June 25th Newman says:

> I don't think we can get a right view of infallibility (as negative more than positive) till we *begin* with the idea of *teaching*.

And in a letter to Isy Froude dated April 24th 1875 Newman writes:

I should say that the word "infallibility" has never been ascribed to the Church in any authoritative document till the Vatican Council. . . . Yet the Church *acted* as infallible from the first. What was the case with the Church was the case with the Pope. The most *real* expression of the doctrine is not that he is infallible but that his decisions are "irreformabilia" and true. So that the question did not arise in the mind of Christians in any formal shape "is he infallible, and in what and how far?" for all they felt was that what he said was "the voice of the Church", "the Church spoke in him", and what the Church spoke was *true*.

(It may be noted here that the encyclical "Humanae Vitae" is manifestly *not* "the voice of the Church" since it deals with an issue on which the Church, both hierarchy and faithful, is seriously divided.)

A satisfactory solution of the problem of the papal primacy, to which the problem of papal infallibility is subsidiary, must surely lie in an accommodation between the Conciliarist and Ultramontane viewpoints. One is fully justified, as a Catholic, in speaking of the primacy as a problem, since Paul VI himself has said in a public allocution that he is conscious that the Chair of Peter, which should be a focus of unity, is today an obstacle to Christian unity. He was thinking of the Eastern and other separated churches; but now, since "Humanae Vitae", the Chair of Peter has become a source and occasion of division within the Pope's own immediate flock, the Latin Church. So much so that, in his sermon in the basilica of St John Lateran on Maundy Thursday 1969, His Holiness spoke of "a ferment practically of schism" within the Church.

In its teaching on collegiality the Second Vatican Council has taken preliminary steps towards a better formulation of the relationship between the Pope and the bishops and the rest of the Church. Section 22 of the Constitution on the Church ("Lumen Gentium") says:

Just as, by the Lord's will, St Peter and the other Apostles constituted one apostolic college, so in a similar way the Roman

Pontiff, as the successor of St Peter, and the bishops as the successors of the apostles, are joined together. . . . But the college or body of bishops has no authority unless it is simultaneously conceived of in terms of its head, the Roman Pontiff, St Peter's successor, and without any lessening of his power of primacy over all, pastors as well as the general faithful. For in virtue of his office, that is as Vicar of Christ, and pastor of the whole Church, the Roman Pontiff has full, supreme, and universal power over the Church. And he can always exercise this power freely.

The order of bishops is the successor to the college of the apostles in teaching authority and pastoral rule. . . . Together with its head, the episcopal order is the subject of supreme and full power over the universal Church. But this power can be exercised only with the consent of the Roman Pontiff. For our Lord made Simon Peter alone the rock and key-bearer of the Church, and appointed him shepherd of the whole flock.

The Council's decree ("Christus Dominus") on the Bishops' Pastoral Office affirms, in section 8, that:

As successors of the apostles, bishops automatically enjoy in the dioceses entrusted to them all the ordinary, proper, and immediate authority required for the exercise of their pastoral office. But this authority never in any instance infringes upon the power which the Roman Pontiff has, by virtue of his office, of reserving cases to himself or to some other authority.

The phrasing of these decrees can give only limited encouragement to those who are disturbed by the present state of imbalance in the hierarchic structure of the Latin Church. But they represent a step forward, away from the old Ultramontane papalism, and are a promise, one hopes, of better things to come, even though they contain much that is bound to ring ominously in the ears of the Orthodox, and of other Christians. The title "Vicar of Christ", as appropriated by the Pope, dates only from the thirteenth century; the older, and more accurate title, was Vicar of St Peter (and of St Paul). For instance, Pope Hadrian I says in a letter addressed to the Emperor: ". . . if you follow the tradition of the orthodox faith of the church of the holy Peter and Paul, the chief Apostles, and embrace their Vicar, as the Emperors who reigned before you . . ."[44] The style Vicar of Christ seems first to have been used by the German emperors. It was also sometimes *applied* to Popes—by St Bernard, for example. It was only *adopted* as a papal style by Innocent III and his successors. Down to the ninth century other bishops called themselves vicars of Christ. The triumphalist title "Roman Pontiff", used to designate the bishop of Rome, is simply a variant of the old pagan imperial title "Pontifex Maximus", which was used satirically of the Bishop of Rome by Tertullian in his *De pudicitia*. It was taken up seriously by the popes as a title of honour in the fifth century. This matter of papal titles has a certain importance because of the attitudes that they reveal.

What strikes one very much in the decrees of Vatican II is their nervous insistence on the *dependence* of the bishops on the Pope. This is especially noticeable in chapter 3 of "Lumen Gentium", which deals with "The Hierarchical Structure of the Church, with special reference to the Episcopate". The bishops are scarcely mentioned without something being subjoined in assertion of the rights of the Holy See; so that, as an Anglican commentator has remarked,[45] "Much of this chapter, which was intended to complement the teaching of Vatican I, sounds like a repetition of it in a more anxious and defensive tone of voice." The same writer points out that the papal primacy is here defended on biblical, historical, and other grounds some of which have in recent years been abandoned as untenable, or at least unreliable, by many Catholic theologians.

Vatican I had defined that when speaking *ex cathedra* on a matter of faith or morals the Pope was endowed with that same infallibility with which Christ willed that his Church should be endowed. The crucial defect of the Constitution "Pastor Aeternus" was that it failed to explain exactly what is the nature of the Church's infallibility which the Pope is said to share. Evidently the Pope's infallibility means something more than "The umpire's decision is final"; but how much more?

Vatican II also has failed to give this vital point the full examination and clarification that it needs. Even now, the doctrine of infallibility is far from being a fully defined article of Church teaching; it is still wide open to examination and clarification. Had this been realised, as it should have been, by those holding authority in the Church, we should not in 1968 have seen bishops and other ecclesiastical superiors dealing out heavy-handed sanctions against priests who knew enough theology to affirm that papal encyclicals were not infallible documents, and that therefore their contents might properly be the subject for respectful dissent and discussion.

However, Vatican II has made a considerable advance in section 25 of the decree "Lumen Gentium", where it says that "This infallibility with which the divine Redeemer willed his Church to be endowed extends as far as the deposit of divine revelation extends, which must be religiously guarded and faithfully expounded"; thereby giving the Church's authoritative approval to the explanation of Monsignor Fessler, which had itself received the informal approval of Pius IX.

THREE

THE POPES AND BIRTH CONTROL

In 1934 the late Father Albert Gille published pseudonymously a little book called "*A Catholic Plea for Reunion* by Father Jerome, R.C. Priest". It was a lively piece of writing, full of good sense, and caused quite a sensation at the time. "Father Jerome" said: "The way Catholics speak of every utterance of the Pope would make one believe that he cannot open his mouth like any sensible man without being the mouthpiece of the Holy Ghost. . . . Now there should be nothing so refreshing as the fact that the Pope can and does put his foot in it when he happens to travel outside the field of pure dogma. . . . Our hero worship is grown into a disease, and there seems to be no reaction possible from within, as our consciences grow daily more sensitive to the slightest suspicion of disloyalty. If this is not stopped, the Popes in a hundred years' time will be as sacred as the Lamas of Tibet, which will be very inconvenient to the Popes, to say the least."

In practice, this state of affairs derives from the long-standing habit of Catholic preachers and apologists of treating almost every papal utterance on every subject under the sun as if it were *quasi-infallible*. There is no justification for this in the decree of 1870, which restricts the Pope's infallibility to his solemn *ex cathedra* pronouncements, for which it lays down clear conditions; but there is plenty of medieval precedent for this attitude. For example, St John Capistran, in a letter written to a fellow Franciscan in 1431, speaks of the Pope as "God's vicar", and says that he is as God (*quasi Deus*) on earth.[1]

The Fathers of the Second Vatican Council have come perilously near to endorsing this point of view in section 25 of "Lumen Gentium", where they distinguish between the Pope's *ex cathedra* teaching and his "authentic" teaching. The passage in question says that

> . . . religious submission of mind and will must be shown in a special way to the authentic teaching of the Roman Pontiff, even when he is not speaking *ex cathedra*. That is, it must be shown in such a way that his supreme magisterium is acknowledged with reverence, the judgements made by him sincerely adhered to, according to his manifest mind and will. His mind and will in the matter may be known chiefly either from his frequent repetition of the same doctrine, or from his manner of speaking.

No attempt is made here to define what is meant by "authentic teaching", but in the common estimation of theologians it is certainly held to include encyclical letters. If *they* are not to be considered as conveying "authentic" teaching, it is difficult to know what is. Nor is "religious submission of mind and will" defined; but it must certainly indicate some kind of *assent*; and if the will comes into it the implication would seem to be that if a Catholic is sincerely unable to agree with a papal statement covering matters outside the area of the papal infallibility, he must nevertheless force himself to accept such teaching.

This apparently was the view of an English priest, a minor prelate of the papal court, who began by publicly dissenting from the encyclical "Humanae Vitae" and then had second thoughts, after which, in a letter to the Catholic press, he retracted from his position and said: "May I give advice to priests who find they cannot give intellectual assent to the encyclical? They are official spokesmen for the Pope and their bishop and can in good conscience promulgate such teaching." This could only mean that in matters not coming within the area of infallibility the consciences of priests were to be handed over to the Pope.

No doubt this would have commended itself to the Archbishop of Cardiff, who in a pastoral letter to his people had said: "If this encyclical has proved anything, it has proved that in these matters of interpreting the natural law all honesty, all compassion, all erudition, all theological acumen is of little account." That is, the utterances of the papal oracle may not be questioned.

Undoubtedly, many of those who hold the "oracular" view of the papal office really do believe this. It was the view of my own higher religious superior in August 1968 who told me, a few days before "Humanae Vitae" was published, that there could be no possibility of dissent from its ruling; most of the members of the religious order to which I belong appeared to subscribe to it; and it was the common view of many bishops. Hence the outbursts of astonishment, and the instant resort to repressive measures, when a number of priests in August 1968 publicly declared their conscientious inability to accept the teaching of "Humanae Vitae". In the event, all these measures, or nearly all of them, failed, and the right to freedom of conscience for Catholics in the area of non-infallible papal statements was quickly and decisively vindicated.

This newly won freedom within the Catholic Church derives from the principle, which only a few years ago it would have been temerarious to hold, that the voice of the Pope when he is not speaking *ex cathedra* is not necessarily the voice of the Church.

Lord Acton put the matter clearly over a hundred years ago.[2] But he was almost a lone voice in England at the time. Writing about the case of Dr Froschammer, a German theologian who had been excommunicated for his writings on theories of pre-existence and against the direct creation by God of the individual soul, Acton said that a man like Froschammer could, when censured,

in the first place yield to an external submission either for the sake of discipline or because his conviction is too weak to support him against the weight of authority; but if the question at issue is more important than the preservation of peace, and if his conviction is strong, he inquires whether the authority that condemns him utters the voice of the Church. If he finds that it does he yields to it or else ceases to profess the faith of Catholics; if he finds that it does not, that it is only the voice of authority, he owes it to his conscience and to the supreme claims of truth to remain constant to that which he believes, in spite of opposition. No authority has power to impose error, and if it resists the truth, the truth must be upheld until it is admitted.

And in a letter printed in *The Times* on November 8th 1874 Acton wrote:

There has been, and I believe there is still, some exaggeration in the idea men form of the agreement in thought and deed which authority can accomplish. As far as decrees, censures and persecution could commit the Court of Rome, it was committed to a denial of the Copernican system. Nevertheless, the history of astronomy shows a whole catena of distinguished Jesuits. It is not the unpropitious times only, but the very nature of things, that protect Catholicism from the consequences of some theories that have grown up within it.

A pertinent passage in Lercher's *Institutiones Theologicae* (vol. 1, section 499: Barcelona 1945) says: "The Holy Spirit will bring it about that the Church will never fall into error because of an encyclical. More probably he will do this by seeing to it that the head of the Church will not issue an erroneous statement. However, it is not absolutely out of the question that he will prevent the error by virtue of its being detected by the subjects of the Pope and their ceasing to give it an internal assent." "Lercher" is a standard manual of divinity; unfortunately it is not widely used in the theological seminaries of Great Britain.

As long as encyclical letters were treated as if they were quasi-infallible, so that to criticise them was considered scarcely compatible with orthodoxy, it was impossible for such mistaken ideas as they might from time to time contain to be identified, except very slowly. If, for example, the reasoning behind

Pius XI's condemnation of contraception in his encyclical of 1930, "Casti Connubii", had been closely studied, Catholics ought to have been able even then to have seen how unsatisfactory it was. Anglicans, who were not fettered by the kind of thought control that operated in the Catholic Church, abandoned this kind of thinking at the Lambeth Conference of the same year.

In 1968, when the encyclical "Humanae Vitae" excited widespread protest from Catholics, the Church authorities would have done well to have been more restrained in their reactions; for if they had thought back to what they had been taught, or had discovered for themselves, in their student days, they would have remembered that in the course of the Church's history there had been more than one example of solemn papal statements and declarations being quietly discarded after being found more or less untenable. Here are just a few.

Pope Gregory II approved the practice, authorised by St Benedict, of "offering" children in monasteries. This offering was the equivalent of monastic profession, and was binding for life. The Church subsequently realised that this practice was contrary to natural justice.

Gregory XI (1370–1378) approved slavery when, in a dispute with the city of Florence, he decreed that any Florentine, wherever he might be found, should become the slave of his captor.

Urban V (1309–1370) dissolved the marriage—a consummated marriage—of Duke Barnabò Visconti of Milan in 1363 on the grounds of the Duke's heresy and unbelief.

In 1185 Urban III, affirming the standard teaching on the ethics of interest in his letter "Consuluit nos", taught that merchants who charged a higher price for goods sold on credit than for those purchased with cash were guilty of the sin of usury and must make restitution.

In 1302 Boniface VIII in the famous bull "Unam Sanctam" said: "We declare, pronounce, and define, that it is absolutely necessary for salvation that every human creature be subject to the Roman Pontiff." What theologian today would care to defend this proposition?

In 1832 Gregory XVI, in his encyclical "Mirari Vos",

condemned the doctrine that every man has a right to freedom of conscience as "an erroneous opinion, or rather a delirium" (*erronea sententia seu potius deliramentum*). The Second Vatican Council has now proclaimed the exact opposite.

In 1860, in his letter "Cum Catholica Ecclesia", Pius IX said that the papal monarchy had been "most wisely determined by God himself", and spoke of "the civil principality with which God has willed that the see of blessed Peter be provided". This was virtually to make God responsible for the False Decretals and the Donation of Constantine.

Pius XI in "Divini illius Magistri" (1929) condemned co-education as fallacious, and repugnant to Christianity. Today public schools conducted by monks are taking girl pupils as well as boys.

The same Pope taught in "Quadragesimo Anno" (1931) that even a mitigated form of socialism was incompatible with Christianity. It was a contradiction in terms to speak of a religious or Christian socialism. "No one can be at the same time a genuine Catholic and a true Socialist."

Pius XII in "Humani Generis" (1950) affirmed that Christians are obliged to believe in the existence of an individual man called Adam as the founder of the human race, and may not hold that "Adam was the name given to some group of our primordial ancestors". Today, not only does it seem biologically more probable that mankind had a polygenistic origin, but it is a commonplace for theologians to admit it.

In "Mystici Corporis" (1943) Pius XII taught that the Mystical Body of Christ and the Roman Catholic Church are to be identified, and he reaffirmed this in "Humani Generis". This doctrine has been discarded by Vatican II.

In "Humani Generis" again the same Pope taught that it is not to be supposed that "a position advanced in an encyclical letter does not *ipso facto* command assent", because such statements are covered by Christ's promise "He that heareth you heareth me" (Luke x, 16). It must be clear, he says, that even though popes are not exercising their authority to the full in encyclical letters, the matters dealt with "can no longer be regarded as a matter of free debate among theologians". This is simply an assertion of the "oracular" idea of papal authority, which today lies in ruins as a result of "Humanae Vitae".

Another difficulty about encyclicals is that they are seldom written by the illustrious authors whose names are attached to them. Modern popes, like most other modern bishops, are seldom theologians in a professional sense; hence their encyclicals are drafted by supposed experts, and are signed by the Pope when they have reached a form that satisfies him. This means that their teaching may be unduly influenced by the views of the theologian who is in favour with the Pope at the moment. Pius XI's birth control encyclical, "Casti Connubii", was put together by the Belgian moral theologian Vermeersch; and "Humanae Vitae" was in part the work of another Belgian Jesuit, Gustav Martelet, who immediately after the encyclical was published said in an interview that the degree to which the document's ruling was binding upon individual Catholics was "a matter for their own consciences."

In his television interview with David Frost on December 6th 1968 Cardinal Heenan said that if he were pope he would be "very careful about writing encyclicals". What we need, in fact, is much fewer of these documents, and that they should be officially identified as interim *ad hoc* statements issued for the guidance of the faithful, to be received with respect and carefully considered by those to whom they are addressed, but not vested with quasi-oracular and semi-infallible status. In other words, it ought no longer to be claimed for them, even if only implicitly, that they proceed from the Church's solemn dogmatic teaching authority. The history of encyclical letters shows all too clearly that such claims cannot be made with safety, and only result, in the end, in a weakening of papal authority, as well as involving Catholics in problems of conscience with which they ought not to be burdened.

With regard to the present birth control controversy, it is puzzling that ecclesiastics should have any difficulty in seeing that laws which all the world rejects are not worth anything but abrogating.

On October 10th 1968 *The Times* published a short letter signed by fifty priests (among them one Benedictine, eight Dominicans, one Jesuit, one Carmelite, one Passionist, and one Assumptionist) saying that they were unable, according to their consciences, to give "loyal internal and external obedience to the view that all (artificial) means of contraception are wrong."

Naturally, in a short letter to a daily paper the signatories were unable to give their reasons for their dissent from the papal ruling; they wished only to make public the fact of their dissent. But their reasons will have been much the same as those given by some ninety American theologians who declared their dissent in a statement published in Washington on July 30th of the same year. The number of those who subscribed to this statement has since risen to six hundred. Severe disciplinary measures were meted out to the original signatories by the American bishops; but in April 1969 the academic senate of the Catholic University at Washington cleared twenty-five of their professors who had signed the document from any wrong-doing. The senate found that the statement signed by the professors was "adequately supported by theological scholarship", and that in composing and issuing the statement the professors "did not violate . . . commitments to the university or to the academic or theological communities."

The statement is worth reprinting as a concise, adequate summary of the reasons why so many priests find it impossible to subscribe to the teaching of "Humanae Vitae". The statement says:

As Roman Catholic theologians we respectfully acknowledge a distinct rôle of hierarchical *magisterium* (teaching authority) in the Church of Christ. At the same time, Christian tradition assigns theologians the special responsibility of evaluating and interpreting pronouncements of the *magisterium* in the light of the total theological data operative in each question or statement. We offer these initial comments on Pope Paul VI's encyclical on the regulation of birth.

The encyclical is not an infallible teaching. History shows that a number of statements of similar or even greater authoritative weight have subsequently been proven inadequate or even erroneous. Past authoritative statements on religious liberty, interest-taking, the right to silence, and the ends of marriage, have all been corrected at a later date.

Many positive values concerning marriage are expressed in Paul VI's encyclical. However, we take exception to the ecclesiology implied and the methodology used by Paul VI in the writing and promulgation of the document. They are incompatible with the Church's authentic self-awareness as expressed in and suggested by the acts of the Second Vatican Council itself. The encyclical consistently assumes that the Church is identical with the hierarchical office. No real importance is afforded to the witness of the life of the Church in its totality; the special witness of many Catholic couples is neglected; it fails to acknowledge the witness of Christian churches and ecclesial communities; it is insensitive to the witness of many men of good will; it pays insufficient attention to the ethical import of modern science. Furthermore, the encyclical betrays a narrow and positivistic notion of papal authority, as illustrated by the rejection of the conclusions of a large part of the international Catholic theological community.

Likewise, we take exception to some of the specific ethical conclusions contained in the encyclical. They are based on an inadequate concept of natural law; the multiple forms of natural law theory are ignored, and the fact that competent philosophers come to different conclusions on this very question is disregarded. Even the minority report of the papal commission noted grave difficulty in attempting to present conclusive proof of the immorality of artificial contraception based on natural law. Other defects include: over-emphasis on the biological aspects of conjugal relations as ethically normative; undue stress on sexual acts and on the faculty of sex viewed in itself apart from the person and the couple; a static world-view which downplays the historical and evolutionary character of humanity in its finite existence as described in Vatican II's Pastoral Constitution on the Church in the Modern World; unfounded assumptions about "the evil consequences of methods of artificial birth control"; indifference to Vatican II's assertion that prolonged sexual abstinence may cause "faithfulness to be imperilled and its quality of fruitfulness be ruined"; and almost total disregard for the dignity of millions of human beings brought into the world without the slightest possibility of being fed and educated decently.

In actual fact, the encyclical demonstrates no development over the teaching of Pius XI's *Casti Connubii*, whose conclusions have been called into question for grave and serious reasons. These reasons, given a muffled voice at Vatican II, have not been adequately handled by the mere repetition of past teaching.

It is common teaching in the Church that Catholics may dissent from authoritative, non-infallible teachings of the *magisterium* when sufficient reasons for so doing exist.

Therefore, as Roman Catholic theologians conscious of our duty and our limitations, we conclude that spouses may reasonably decide according to their conscience that artificial contraception in some circumstances is permissible and indeed necessary to preserve and foster the values and sacredness of marriage.

It is our conviction also that true commitment to the mystery of Christ and the Church requires a candid statement of mind at this time by all Catholic theologians.

Until 1965 it was taken for granted by Catholics, including most priests, that the teaching of Pope Pius XI on birth control, as formulated in his encyclical "Casti Connubii", represented exactly what the Church had always taught. No one could be blamed for thinking so. This was the official party line, and there was no evidence at all readily available to the contrary. If the ordinary priest consulted his *Denzinger*[3] for earlier papal statements on birth control he could find practically nothing.

This situation was changed completely in 1965 by the publication of Dr John T. Noonan's book *Contraception: a history of its treatment by the Catholic theologians and canonists*,[4] which showed how much Catholic thought had varied on this subject, and what varying, and often very strange, influences had shaped the theologians' views from age to age.

Every Catholic is familiar with the assertion that contraception "has always been condemned" by the Church. Of certain forms of contraception this is manifestly true, but as a "blanket" statement the assertion is inadequate. The assertion "It has always been condemned" has been readily accepted, without scrutiny, by those for whom, because of a faulty ecclesiology, the Pope is an oracle which cannot contradict itself, or even modify in any significant way its previous vaticinations. A letter in *The Tablet* of October 19th 1968 from Dr C. H. Talbot, written from the Wellcome Institute of the History of Medicine, discussed the attitude of the Early and Medieval Church to the practice of contraception between married partners. Medieval doctors took their teaching on gynaecology from Hippocrates and other classical writers. These pagan writers viewed contraception simply as a prophylactic method of avoiding certain dangers in child-bearing, and medieval physicians took the same view.

In the eleventh and twelfth centuries translations of Arab medical works by Avicenna and others appeared in the west. Their writings, which treated at length of methods of contraception, were widely circulated, and were used in university curricula throughout Europe. The universities were under clerical control, and clerical teachers were prominent in the medical faculties. There is no record of any condemnation by the Church authorities either of the use of these treatises or of the information about contraception which they contained. It seems that everyone took for granted that the use of certain contraceptive measures *by married people for reasons of health* involved no moral problem. Dr Talbot concludes: "When one considers that some of these medical teachers afterwards became bishops, like Arundel of Chichester, and that whereas in their synods they could legislate about clerics entering a tavern or playing games, they make no mention of the practice of contraception, one begins to wonder about the assertion that 'it has always been condemned'."

The crucial passage of "Casti Connubii", which has been held to restate the Church's unswerving teaching as held from the earliest times, reads as follows:

Assuredly, no reason, even the most serious, can make congruent with nature, and decent, what is intrinsically against nature. Since the act of husband and wife is by its own nature ordered to the generation of offspring, those who in its exercise deliberately deprive it of its natural force and power act against nature and effect what is base and intrinsically shameful. . . .

The Catholic Church, to whom God himself has committed the integrity and decency of morals, now standing amid this moral ruin, raises her voice aloud through our mouth, in sign of her divine mission, in order to keep the chastity of the nuptial bond free from this foul error, and again promulgates:

Any use whatever of marriage in the exercise of which the act is deprived by human effort of its natural power of procreating life, violates the law of God and nature; and those who do such a thing are stained by a grave and mortal sin.

The Pope intended the encyclical in part as an answer to the statement of the Anglican bishops at the 1930 Lambeth Conference, in part as a reply to some German Catholics who had been asking, in the magazine *Hochland*, for a revision of previous teaching on this matter.

At the 1930 Lambeth Conference, in spite of the determined opposition of a minority led by Bishop Gore, the following resolution had been carried by 193 votes to 67 (with 47 abstensions):

Where there is a clearly felt moral obligation to limit or avoid parenthood, the method must be decided on Christian principles. The primary and obvious method is complete abstinence from intercourse (as far as may be necessary) in a life of discipline and self-control lived in the power of the Holy Spirit. Nevertheless in those cases where there is such a clearly-felt moral obligation to limit or avoid parenthood, and where there is a morally sound reason for avoiding complete abstinence, the Conference agrees that other methods may be used, provided that this is done in the light of the same Christian principles. The Conference records its strong condemnation of the use of any methods of conception control from motives of selfishness, luxury, or mere convenience.

The principal author of the encyclical "Casti Connubii" was the Jesuit theologian Arthur Vermeersch. He was seventy-two years old at the time, and regarded birth control as a world-wide menace. Noonan says that he had been stung by a reference in the Lambeth Conference statement to the teaching of St Alphonsus Liguori, one of the most reputed of Catholic theologians and a Doctor of the Church, on the question of good faith in this particular matter. St Alphonsus recognised that there are some circumstances under which the rigid maintenance of moral principle may be impossible.

As long previously as 1909 Vermeersch had been the dominant influence behind Cardinal Mercier's pastoral letter on "A Grave Moral Peril", i.e., birth control; he was concerned also in the drafting of an instruction put out by the Belgian bishops for the guidance of parish priests. It was noted at the time by another Belgian theologian, de Smedt, that there were people to be found who believed in good faith that contraception, used for serious reasons, was not sinful. It was de Smedt's opinion that if a confessor thought that questioning such people would have no effect on their conduct, it was best that they should be left alone. This was not the general opinion among theologians, and certainly it was not that of Father Vermeersch, who believed that "in areas where contraception flourished, the general rule should be discreet inquiry about the fulfilment of the obligations of marriage".

The few readers of "Casti Connubii" who were versed in the history of moral theology must have wondered at the contrast between the severity of its teaching and the gentle answers given by the Roman Sacred Penitentiary to questions on this subject in 1842. In that year John-Baptist Bouvier, Bishop of Le Mans, had put these three questions to the Penitentiary:

1. Do couples who use marriage in such a way as to avoid conception commit an intrinsically evil act?
2. If the act is held to be intrinsically evil, can couples not

accusing themselves of it in confession be considered as being in good faith, excusing them from grave fault?

3. Should approval be given to the conduct of those confessors who, for fear of offending married couples, do not question them about the way in which they exercise their marital rights?

The Sacred Penitentiary's answer to the first question said that co-operation by the wife in such action was in certain circumstances permissible. Nothing was said as to the husband's part, but it seemed to be implied that his action was sinful.

The answers to questions 2 and 3 were very lenient. Confessors should keep in mind the teaching of St Alphonsus on such matters; wives may be asked "whether they have paid the marital debt", but "about other things, be silent unless asked."

Noonan remarks that "It seems probable that Bouvier, himself a follower of Liguori, put the questions to the Penitentiary with some assurance that its answers would be given on Liguorian principles. The Penitentiary thereby gave tacit approval to confessors who did not lose penitents by questioning them about contraception. It accepted the position that contraception could be practised in innocence of its malice. In face of the description of a diocese where the practice was widespread, the Penitentiary did not consider the social evil to be such that education should be attempted in the confessional."[5]

This tolerant reply of the Roman Penitentiary may have encouraged moralists such as Bouvier, and Thomas Gousset, Cardinal Archbishop of Rheims, who held similar views, to think that the Church might be going to follow its recent quiet change of front in the matter of the ethics of interest with a parallel shift of emphasis in the matter of contraception. But in fact no such shift was to occur for another century and a quarter; and then the change would not come through any pronouncement from Rome, but as the result of a process of rethinking which was taking place in the Church at all levels.

Under Pius IX there was a return to a firmer position, when the Congregation of the Inquisition in 1851 condemned two propositions concerning marriage and contraception as "scandalous, erroneous, and contrary to the natural law of marriage". Noonan characterises the Inquisition's reply as "comparatively restrained". The propositions were condemned as "erroneous", but not as heretical. This meant that they were to be regarded as untrue in terms of orthodox theology, but not formally contrary to the faith.

At one time contraception—but the reference was not normally to its use by married couples for grave reasons of health—had been considered as equivalent to homicide. This was the teaching of a text known from its opening words as *Si aliquis*, first issued in an early penitential, or book of instructions to confessors, and later incorporated by Burchard, a tenth–eleventh century Bishop of Rheims, into his *Decretum*, or collection of canon law. Noonan says that *Si aliquis* was preserved in the Church's law down to the publication of the new *Codex Iuris Canonici* in 1917; but its interpretation and application varied. Authorities of such importance as, for instance, St Antoninus of Florence, Denis the Carthusian, and Dominic Soto, make no mention of it in their manuals. On the other hand, Cajetan, fifteenth–sixteenth century Dominican and cardinal, and theologian of the first rank, invokes it. The Roman Catechism of 1566, intended for the instruction of the people, equates contraception with homicide. The Catechism, however, restricted the context to that of contraceptive medicines, and did not support St Bernardine of Siena and others in classifying coitus interruptus as homicide.

The high-water mark of Roman severity was reached with the bull *Effraenatam* of Sixtus V (October 29th 1588). This went beyond both the Roman Catechism and *Si aliquis* by treating the giving or taking of contraceptives as equivalent to murder both in canon law and in the civil law of the States of the Church. Such actions were made subject to an excommunication from which only the Holy See could absolve the guilty party, even if the offender were actually dying.

These are the severest penalties ever invoked by any authority, whether lay or ecclesiastical, against the practice of contraception. Pope Sixtus died in 1590, and a few months later his successor, Gregory XIV, repealed all the penalties prescribed by the bull except those applying to the abortion of a forty-day-old foetus. In the decree of annulment, *Sedes Apostolica*, it was declared that the decree *Effraenatam* was "to be held in this part as if it had never been issued".

Father Vermeersch, the ghost-writer of "Casti Connubii", held that the passage in the encyclical which condemned birth control was infallible in virtue of an *ex cathedra* exercise of the Pope's teaching authority. After all, Pius XI had spoken, or rather written, solemnly, as the earthly head of the Church, and in so doing he had promulgated once again moral doctrine which he claimed "had been transmitted from the beginning". Other theologians, however, among them the distinguished Jesuit moralist Father Creusen, held that in "promulgating" the doctrine the Pope was not making a definition, but only reaffirming the Church's supposedly unchanging teaching. On this view, to deny the doctrine would not involve loss of faith, but would be a sin "against the virtue of faith".

To such subtleties had the unsatisfactory and uncompleted infallibility definition of 1870 led the theologians. The faithful, however, knew nothing of such nice distinctions, and everywhere in the Church the Pope's condemnation of birth control was looked on as infallible, or as nearly so as made no difference. In such circumstances it was natural that the reasoning which the Pope adduced in support of his condemnation should not have been given any very close examination.

Recently it has been argued that a strict interpretation of the language of "Casti Connubii" would limit its condemnation to coitus interruptus and the use of condoms, both of which vitiate the sexual act in its exercise; but it is now too late in the day to advance so restrictive an interpretation, since the broader view, which sees in it a condemnation of all "artificial" methods of contraception, has held the field since 1930 and long ago received the august sanction of Pius XII. But its meaning can hardly be forced to cover oral contraceptives, which were unknown in 1930. The pill is not specifically mentioned in "Humanae Vitae" (nor is any other method of contraception); section 14 seems to condemn it, when it says that "Similarly [to the use of contraceptives] is excluded any action which either before, at the moment of, or after sexual intercourse, is specifically intended to prevent pro-creation—whether as an end or as a means."

However that may be, one certain result of the reinforcement by "Humanae Vitae" of the teaching of "Casti Connubii" is that innumerable Catholic couples who are not prepared to disobey the Pope's ruling, and who for one reason or another cannot use the so-called "rhythm" method, which paradoxically the Church allows, will be forced back on to the oldest of all methods of birth control: coitus interruptus. As well as being the oldest, this is also the most unreliable method, and the most physiologically and psychologically damaging.

This is hardly, one imagines, what the conservatives of the Vatican had in view when they persuaded the Pope to sign this unhappy document.

It may fairly be called an unhappy document irrespective of whether one agrees with its teaching on birth control or not. It is an unhappy document from the circumstances of its compilation and publication, in that it was issued by the Pope *motu proprio* just after Vatican II had declared and stressed the collegial nature of Church government; the advice of the papal commission on birth control, from which only four of its sixty-odd members dissented, was ignored, no adequate reasons being assigned for its rejection; such few arguments as the encyclical contains in support of the papal ruling have failed to carry general conviction among Catholics; and these arguments are themselves based on a philo-sophy of natural law, whereas the four dissenting members of the commission, all of them priests, had declared their total inability to justify their opposition to the majority findings on a natural law basis.

The encyclical's final draft appears to have been hurriedly and carelessly written[6] in Italian, which explains in part the in-adequacies of the Latin and English translations. The two sections (7 and 10) which reflect the newer theology of marriage are lifted from the commission's majority report without acknowledge-ment, but in general the whole encyclical represents a retreat from, if not an actual contradiction of, the teaching of Vatican II in the

Constitution "Gaudium et Spes". It contains one section (13) which is incoherent in Latin, Italian, or English. Paragraph 14 brackets together abortion, sterilisation, and contraception, placing them all on the same level, although the Pope had been warned by one of his advisers, Dr Joseph Fuchs S.J., not to confuse these issues.

The Latin Church, in marked contrast with the Eastern, has for centuries been excessively preoccupied with moralising, and has taught, in practice, a static, rule-of-law morality which is unable to move forward openly in the light of new insights, new situations, and a new understanding of human nature. Western Christianity has tended to present God's principal activity as that of issuing commands; so that morality becomes chiefly a matter of obeying orders, more specifically a matter of what men ought not to do: something negative.

One difficulty about equating morality with the observance of commands issued by God is fairly obvious. How can we be certain that God does in fact command, or prohibit, this or that? Hitler constantly invoked the name of God as sanction for his policies; and apparently sincerely. Dr Vervoerd and his followers, most of them Christians, have claimed that the policy of *apartheid* is according to the will of God; slavery has in the past been defended by Christians as being part of God's eternal plan for mankind; Catholic theologians have approved the use of nuclear weapons as a lawful means for defending Christian civilisation; and the authority of God has frequently been invoked in justification of capital punishment, and also of corporal punishment: that is, of the use of violence against children who are too small to retaliate. The use of anaesthetics, especially in childbirth, was once widely believed to be against the will of God. One could give many more such instances.

It is useless for the Catholic to say, "Yes, the human conscience is fallible and may be mistaken; this is where the Church comes in. The Church has been set up to tell us with infallible certainty what God actually does command or prohibit." A slight acquaintance with history is enough to make one see that the Church has often been a very poor guide in matters of morality. The treatment of

Jews, the use of torture against suspected heretics, the employment of *castrati* in the papal choir, the papal medal struck to commemorate the Massacre of St Bartholomew, all these things have been taken for granted by devout churchmen as being in accordance with God's law; and whereas contraception has been denounced by them *ad nauseam*, rarely is a word heard from the pulpit or in pastoral letters in condemnation of war, genocide, vivisection, or capital and corporal punishment.

It was long taught as common doctrine in the Church that a Catholic could not be a conscientious objector to military service. This scandal has not been altogether removed by the somewhat timid words of the Second Vatican Council on the subject.

It is especially curious that the present Pope, who has taken such a harsh line in the matter of contraception, seems to have given positive encouragement to doctors engaged in operations involving the transplanting of bodily organs from one human being to another: a matter which would appear to raise moral problems far more complex than those connected with contraception.

All these matters, since they have no connexion with the Christian revelation, come within the area of the Church's "ordinary" teaching authority, and therefore cannot be the subject of "infallible" pronouncements. In the Church's attitude to such questions, therefore, there is likely to be an observable process of development and clarification. But at least since 1870 Catholics have been so bemused by a distorted and ultramontane view of the Church's infallibility that they have tended *not to think* about moral problems, but simply to accept as infallibly right the common teaching of theologians, most of whom live lives that are quite remote from the circumstances which impose upon modern man his moral dilemmas. In any case, the judgements of moral theologians are based largely on precedent, and on principles which may not have been subjected to any rigid scrutiny since the thirteenth century or even earlier.

As long as the *ecclesia docens* and the *ecclesia discens* (the teaching church and the learning church) are regarded as virtually separate bodies, this state of affairs is likely to continue. Morality, which springs from a few fundamental and eternal principles, is a flexible, subtle, evolving thing; *Christian* morality should derive from the Gospel and from the pooling of the knowledge and experience of *all* the members of the Church.

The rightness or wrongness of human actions is determined by the nature of the actions themselves, the intention of the person who performs them, and the circumstances in which they take place. The basic rule of natural morality is that good must be done and evil avoided; but life is not as simple as that. How do we know what *is* good here and now? Everyone knows that stealing is wrong; we also know that if a starving man helps himself to someone else's food, since it is the only food available, his action is not blameworthy.

For Christians—but of course not for Christians only—good actions are *loving* actions. If a husband knows that his wife will probably die, leaving her children motherless, if she has another child, or that her health will suffer serious damage if she has another child here and now, or that more children at this point will mean the family getting hopelessly into debt, with all the damaging consequences that must follow, does he act wrongly if he takes steps to avoid these calamities? What these steps shall be the husband and wife must determine according to their consciences, in view of their particular circumstances. For a long time the Church said that total sexual abstinence was the only morally licit means; then the use of the "safe" period was admitted, at first grudgingly. But for many couples neither of these solutions is practicable.

This is not arguing from hard cases, because hard cases, in the sense of unusual cases, are rare. These situations, on the contrary, are the common, everyday experience of innumerable people.

In this sense all ethics are situation ethics, and necessarily so. The only situation ethics that must be excluded is that which denudes morality of all principle and makes it simply a matter of pleasure, convenience, or convention.

In a letter published in *The Tablet* on March 15th 1969 the Archbishop of Durban said that "Catholic moral theology abounds in a certain kind of situationism: not the situationism that denies objective moral values, but the situationism that admits that objective moral values may clash in certain circumstances and that we need principles to guide us in resolving the apparent clash."

The Archbishop has rendered a valuable service in questioning the traditional understanding of the principle that the end cannot justify the means, which he thinks has so mesmerised Catholic moralists that they have sometimes persuaded themselves that they were not justifying the means by the end, when in fact they were.

He gives as an example the fact that we take it for granted that it is wrong to perform an operation for the removal of a womb without necessity, and that it is a thousand times more wrong if the womb contains a living foetus. But if there is a sufficiently good end—such as saving a woman's life threatened by cancer of the womb—the operation is held to be justified on the principle of double effect.[7] But this really amounts to saying that certain actions which are held to be wrong "in themselves", such as the destruction of a living foetus or the killing of non-combatants in a war, are lawful *if there is a justifying end*.

As the Archbishop says, this is an area of moral theology that needs "a thorough re-examination". It includes the question of actions that are supposed to be "intrinsically evil". To say that a human action is intrinsically evil would seem to imply that there are certain human actions whose morality cannot be affected either by the intention of the one who performs them or by the circumstances in which they are done. Is this really possible?

It is curious how in the Catholic Church the principle of "development" in *doctrine* has been so readily admitted, while in the field of *moral* theology it has scarcely been recognised. Where it has been applied, as in the ethics of interest, it has been applied tacitly, and with the minimum of comment.

Ultramontane ways of thinking have invaded this area also, so that for the great mass of Catholics morality is thought of as something that is *imposed* by the Church's teaching authority, which in practice means the Pope, for General Councils have not been much concerned with moral questions, and in any case meet only infrequently. But the *teaching* church is really only another aspect of the *learning* church, that is, the *whole* church, clergy and faithful together. This is the view that Newman was insinuating in his essay *On Consulting the Faithful in Matters of Doctrine*, an essay which got him into a good deal of trouble. In it Newman affirmed that while "the gift of discerning, discriminating, defining, promulgating, and enforcing any portion of Christian teaching rests solely in the *Ecclesia docens*", nevertheless, "the body of the faithful is one of the witnesses of revealed doctrine", and that "their consensus throughout Christendom is the voice of the Infallible Church".

Within certain limits this has always been recognised; but the principle has been interpreted far too narrowly. The great sixteenth-century Jesuit, and Doctor of the Church, St Robert Bellarmine says (*De Romano Pontifice* iv, 7):

> For even though the Pope is infallible, he ought not to neglect the use of human and ordinary means by which he may arrive at knowledge of the real truth concerning the matter under discussion. But the ordinary means for this purpose is a Council, greater or smaller, according to the greater or smaller importance of the subject-matter.

The teaching of Vatican I is the same. Section 4 of the Constitution "Pastor Aeternus" says that in times past

> the Roman Pontiffs, according to the exigencies of times and circumstances, sometimes assembling Ecumenical Councils, or asking for the mind of the Church scattered throughout the world, sometimes by particular Synods, sometimes using other helps which Divine Providence supplied, defined as to be held those things which, with the help of God, they had recognised as conformable with the Sacred Scriptures and Apostolic Tradition.

It may reasonably be supposed that in inserting this statement the Fathers of the First Vatican Council had in mind to exclude the possibility of papal infallibility being understood in an oracular sense.

Bellarmine insists that before he exercises his teaching authority in a grave matter the Pope will use the "ordinary and human means" such as we all use when we are trying to get at the truth about something. He takes it for granted that the Pope will *discuss* the matter at issue in a Council, "greater or smaller". The removal of the birth control question from the agenda of the Second Vatican Council seems to have been a serious blunder.

In an interview granted to a representative of the newspaper *Corriere della Sera* on October 3rd 1965 the Pope said:

> We are faced with so many problems. They are so numerous, and we have so many answers to prepare! We wish to speak to the world, and we have to decide day by day on matters which will have consequences throughout the centuries. We must answer the questions of the modern man, the modern Christian, and there are some questions, such as those concerned with the problems of the Christian family, which we find particularly difficult. Take birth control, for example. The world asks for our opinion[8] and we have to find an answer. But what answer? It is impossible to keep silent, but to speak is most difficult. The Church has never, for centuries, had to face such questions. And this is a matter which is extraneous to the life of priests,[9] even causing some natural embarrassment.
>
> So, the Commissions meet and the piles of reports and studies mount up. But at the end of it all, it is we who have to decide. And we are alone in our decision. It is harder to decide than to study. But we must say something. What . . .? We need God's help to enlighten us.

"And we are alone in our decision." But why? The principle of the collegiality of the Pope and the bishops had been affirmed by the Council only a year before. Here, if ever, was an occasion for its exercise. It would be difficult not to sympathise with the Pope in his ordeal; to solve on his own so momentous a problem, fraught with such consequences for the future of the Church, is more than should be required of any one man, however exalted his position, no matter how great his sincerity and his learning.

But why this feverish search for a categorical answer at all? If the Pope had taken wide enough and deep enough soundings he would have found that in the Church at large, among both the clergy and the laity, there was no very marked preponderance of opinion one way or the other. A Gallup Poll taken among the Roman Catholics of Great Britain in August 1968 showed that more than half of them (54 per cent) disapproved of the Pope's ban on birth control. This figure would probably be about right for the Catholics of all countries with a high standard of education. In more culturally backward countries there would probably be a heavier vote the other way; but even in such countries as Italy, Spain, and Ireland it can no longer be taken for granted that most of the inhabitants are automatic conformists who will think and do exactly as Father O'Flaherty or Don Abbondio tells them. The plain fact is that in this particular matter there is as yet no overwhelming *consensus fidelium* either way.

The Pope could very well have said, one would have thought, that since there was nothing in Scripture on this matter, and since there was no general *consensus fidelium*, even a provisionally definitive judgement on the matter was not possible at the present time. Therefore, in view of the widespread criticism throughout the Church of the pronouncements of Pius XI and Pius XII, it could be recognised that for the moment a state of doubt prevailed in the Church on the matter of birth control. Invoking the principle of *Lex dubia non obligat*, therefore, the Pope could have ruled that Catholic married couples were free to follow their own consciences, seriously formed in the light of the general Christian teaching on marriage. This was, in fact, the position that had been pragmatically arrived at during the four years of silence and hesitation; and it is the position that has now received the sanction of numerous bishops' conferences throughout the world.

At least one of the authors of "Humanae Vitae" foresaw what the result of the publication of the encyclical would be, for section 18 of the encyclical says that its teaching will be rejected by many within the Church, but that the Church is not surprised to be a sign of contradiction to many. Yet the Pope was clearly taken aback by the hostile reaction of so many of the clergy and

laity, and even of a few outspoken bishops. One can only specu-
late on the reasons for the Pope's surprise at something that was
certain and inevitable. Under the shock of this unfavourable
reaction from so many of his spiritual children the Pope referred
in a discourse at Bogotà on August 25th 1968 to persons who
"arrogate to themselves the permission to proclaim their own
personal opinions, on which they confer that authority which they
more or less covertly question in him who by divine right
possesses such a protected and awesome charism", and who hold
that "each one in the Church may think and believe what he
wants".

This is not the position at all, and in later pronouncements the
Pope has spoken more understandingly and sympathetically of
those who are unable to assent to the teaching of the encyclical
and who have felt impelled in conscience to make their dissent
known. While not presuming to judge the consciences of others,
those priests who made some kind of public protest did so lest,
by seeming to support the teaching of the encyclical, they should
incur the judgement that awaits those who knowingly impose on
others burdens from which they are free themselves, and which
they do nothing to help others to bear. In so doing it was not in
their minds to make any criticism of their fellow-clergy who
conscientiously accepted the teaching of "Humanae Vitae".

On July 24th 1969 an article was published in the Vatican's
official newspaper *Osservatore Romano* to mark the first anniversary
of "Humanae Vitae". The writer, Padre Ermenegildo Lio OFM,
one of those who had had some share in the drafting of the
encyclical, said: "Whoever does not hear and follow Peter, who
has spoken afresh in manner so categorical, clear and binding,
cannot be an authentic pastor of Christ."

Here again is the old mystical identification of the Pope with
St Peter, which by implication attributes to the Pope divine
inspiration in his utterances and an oracular function in the
Church. The writer of this article made it clear that he considered
that a series of episcopal hierarchies—notably the French, Dutch,
Belgian, German, Scandinavian, Anglo-Welsh, and Canadian—
had betrayed their vocations as pastors of souls through their

failure to impose strict adherence to "Humanae Vitae" on their flocks.

The Synod of Bishops held in Rome in October 1969 has done nothing to resolve this conflict of view between the Holy See and a large proportion of the Catholic episcopate. The question of "Humanae Vitae" was not even raised at the Synod. As a result of the Synod the Pope has, under pressure, made a few small gestures, which he could well afford to, in the direction of collegiality. But fundamentally the situation remains the same. The Synod of Bishops remains an advisory body, with no deliberative powers. As *The Times* correspondent in Rome pointed out in a despatch of October 26th, the agreement between the Pope and the bishops to exchange information in respect of major public statements is largely in the Pope's favour. If he does not like a draft statement submitted by a national hierarchy, he can veto it; but whereas he is now willing to receive advice on the drafting of proposed papal statements, he is under no obligation to follow it.

FOUR

THE MINISTRY

THE publication of the encyclical "Humanae Vitae" has done immense good in that it has brought out into the open the whole question of the nature of Church authority, especially in matters of belief. At the time of the Reformation, when in country after country rebellion broke out against abuses of power in the Latin church, the drawbridge was lowered, and those inside the fortress who still dared to protest were liable, so to speak, to be shot at dawn as traitors. An admirable unity was thus secured; but it was an artificial unity, which was too brittle to last.

Today even the outward unity of Catholicism is shattered. Previously it had always been possible to conceal from the world at large most of the internal tensions and dissensions that went on behind the Latin church's façade of monolithic coherence; this is no longer possible. The cracks in the fabric are now too wide to be papered over, and protest against abuses can no longer be stifled by an autocratic hierarchy. An autocratic papacy means an autocratic episcopate, and an autocratic episcopate means an autocratic priesthood. Autocracy is not necessarily or always harsh; it may take the form of an enlightened paternalism. But paternalism itself is out of favour; the temper of the times is against it.

John XXIII showed us a new kind of pope; or at least a kind of pope that had not been seen for centuries. Gradually, as a result of

Pope John's influence and example, a new kind of bishop is beginning to appear, unautocratic, the friend and father of his clergy and people. A similar change is apparent in the priesthood. The laity can no longer be coerced and ordered about; but they are very willing to be led. Father O'Casey can no longer run the parish single-handed without rendering an account of his stewardship to anyone except the bishop. The parish must be seen as a *community*, a fellowship, in which all—the pastor, his assistant priest or priests, the sisters in the convent, the people in the pews, and even those who have given up coming to church—work together, under the leadership of the parish priest, to build up the kingdom of God in this particular place.

It is understandable that many bishops and priests who have been trained to fulfil an autocratic function are now bewildered to find themselves rejected in this rôle. The Pope is probably no different in this respect from any other priest or bishop. The whole idea of the Christian church's ministry needs to be re-examined and redefined if the priesthood is to play an effective part in the modern church and the modern world, and not survive as just an archaic relic of former days.

In Catholic ecclesiology the Church as a visible institution is governed by officers known as bishops, in communion with the chief bishop, the Bishop of Rome. The word "bishop" is an Anglo-Saxon corruption of the Latin word "episcopus", which is derived from the Greek *episkopos*, meaning "overseer". Bishops are fond of calling themselves the successors of the Apostles. This, as the theologians say, is true *secundum quid*; meaning in due measure, but not literally. The apostolic office was unique, and expired with the death of the last apostle. The authority of Apostles was above that of bishops, and was incommunicable. St Ignatius, Bishop of Antioch, says in his epistle to the Romans: "I am not ordering you, as though I were a Peter or a Paul. They were Apostles, and I am a condemned criminal." The bishops are the guardians of the faith handed down from the Apostles, and in that sense may be said to be their successors.

Ignatius appears to have become Bishop of Antioch, a metropolitan see, about the year 69. He had a high idea of the bishop's office, as may be seen from this passage from his letter to the Christians of Smyrna: "Make sure that no step affecting the church is ever taken by anyone without the bishop's sanction. The sole eucharist you should consider valid is one that is celebrated by the bishop himself, or by some person authorised by him. Where the bishop is to be seen, there let all his people be; just as wherever Jesus Christ is present we have the world-wide church." Whatever criticisms may have been made of individual bishops at different times, reverence for the episcopal office is a permanent characteristic of Catholic Christianity.

The development of the primitive apostolic Christian communities into the Catholic Church (a general expression designating the whole community of orthodox believers, as opposed to the numerous sects and heresies that began to appear even during the lifetime of the Apostles) was rapid. As far as the officers of these first communities were concerned, there seems at first to have been no clear distinction between bishops and another class of church officers called presbyters, or elders. The evidence is obscure, but apparently at first there were several presbyter-bishops in each local community or "church", and it seems probable that the Roman church itself was at first governed by presbyters. But by St Ignatius's time the "monarchic" episcopate —one church, one bishop—seems to have become the rule.

It was the episcopal office, at first plural, later monarchic, which assured to each Christian community its constitution and stability. Batiffol thinks[1] that at first the bishop's powers were purely statutory and juridical, being exercised in the government of the community, while faith and teaching were based on the charisms,[2] and were unconnected with government and administration. When those charisms, such as the working of miracles, which were a transitory phenomenon of the Early Church, ceased, the teaching and ruling functions were combined in the bishop.

The one universal church was thought of as comprising all the many local churches, none of which was reckoned to be entirely autonomous and self-sufficient. Thus the election of a church's bishop was made by the bishops of neighbouring churches, in the presence of the people, who presented the candidates.

In the prologue to St Ignatius's epistle to the Philadelphians we meet for the first time the mention of a church organised on the clear, orderly basis of a threefold ministry of bishops, priests, and deacons. The situation in the early church with regard to the ministry seems to have been somewhat fluid and confused. St Paul, in Philippians i, 1, mentions "bishops and deacons", but says nothing about presbyters; in Titus i, 5–7, he appears to identify presbyters with bishops. It is thought that bishops (overseers) and presbyters (elders) were at first identical, either word being used to denote the same office, and that later one of the presbyter-bishops in each church began to be singled out for a position of special authority, so that eventually the word "bishop" came to denote the "monarchic" bishop only.

Ordination to the episcopate or presbyterate was by a rite which included the imposition of hands. Cf. Acts xiii, 1–3: "Now there were at Antioch, in the church that was there, prophets and teachers. . . . And as they ministered to the Lord and fasted, the Holy Ghost said, Separate me Barnabas and Saul for the work whereunto I have called them. Then, when they had fasted and prayed and laid their hands on them, they sent them away." And in I Timothy iv, 14 St Paul says: "Neglect not the gift that is in thee, which was given thee by prophecy, with the laying on of hands of the presbytery."

There is in the New Testament no fixed and exclusive list of permanent ministries valid for all Christian communities. Some scholars think that there was no ordained ministry in the communities for which St Paul was responsible, since there is no mention of such a thing in his letters to them. In I Corinthians xii, 4–11, Paul gives a list of ministries that have received the Spirit in the church of Corinth. These are: Prophets, Teachers, Workers of miracles, Healers, Helpers, Rulers (Administrators), People with the gift of tongues, and Interpreters.

The institution of the office of deacon is recorded in Acts vi, 1–6. The early Christian writing known as the *Didache*, or The Teaching of the Lord through the Twelve Apostles, written probably soon after A.D. 117, mentions bishops and deacons, together with prophets and teachers, but says nothing of presbyters. The late Dom Gregory Dix thought that the beginning of the period when the historic threefold ministry of bishops, presbyters, and deacons was in possession of the whole field of church order could not be placed much later than *c.* A.D. 160.[3]

Whether or not the episcopal office is of divine institution—and the Council of Trent in canon 6 of its decree on the Sacrament of Order[4] says that it is—it is surely the one order that in the nature of things is morally necessary for the continuance of the Church's life.

In saying that the orders of bishop, priest, and deacon constitute a hierarchy that is of divine institution, the Council of Trent did not define what it meant by "divine institution", and presumably did not mean to imply that no other order besides these could be divinely instituted. At any rate, it did not say so. Exactly what the Council meant by saying that the threefold ministry was of "divine ordination" may be left to theologians to discuss. The Thirty-nine Articles of the Church of England have nothing to say about this; but the Preface to the Form and Manner of Making, Ordaining, and Consecrating Bishops, Priests, and Deacons in the Book of Common Prayer says that "It is evident unto all men diligently reading holy Scripture and ancient Authors, that from the Apostles' time there have been these three Orders of Ministers in Christ's Church: Bishops, Priests, and Deacons."

Presbyterians, who have eliminated bishops from their system of church order out of dislike for prelacy have simply gone back to the primitive state of things in which bishop and presbyter were identical. Presbyterians claim, in fact, that the only true "bishop" is the ordinary parish minister. It has been observed by a former bishop of the Scots Episcopal Church that "the Scottish parish minister and the Anglican incumbent do to a very large extent perform the functions of the primitive bishop."[5]

In practice the Church of England has always maintained a high doctrine of episcopacy, while not denying the spiritual effectiveness of non-episcopal ministries.

In view of the comparatively little that we know about the state of things in the apostolic church it would be difficult to disprove the contention of Archbishop Whitgift in his controversy with the Puritan divine Cartwright:[6]

The substance and matter of government must indeed be taken out of the word of God, and consisteth in these points, that the word be truly taught, the sacraments rightly administered, virtue furthered, vice repressed, and the church kept in quietness and order. The offices in the church, whereby this government is wrought, be not namely and particularly expressed in the scriptures, but in some points left to the discretion and liberty of the church, to be disposed according to times, places, and persons.

Commenting on Richard Hooker's differences of emphasis concerning episcopacy in the earlier and later books of the *Ecclesiastical Polity*, the late Dr Norman Sykes said[7] that "even in these later books, the author is content to ascribe to episcopacy apostolic, not dominical, authority. To Hooker moreover all good forms of polity . . . are established by God. It would seem therefore that to him episcopacy, by reason of its historic tradition from the apostolic age to his own times, had demonstrated its divine authority. But this was very different from the claim that it is the exclusive form of ministry prescribed by the scriptures."

Of the three orders of bishop, priest, and deacon, it is only the episcopal order which is increasing in numbers at the present time. Fewer priests are being ordained every year, and therefore fewer deacons. The number of bishops is increasing in consequence of section 27 of Vatican II's decree ("Christus Dominus"), On the Pastoral Office of Bishops, which allows diocesan bishops to appoint one or more "episcopal vicars" to help them. This new kind of assistant bishop has the same authority as a vicar general, but is more like an Anglican archdeacon in that he is given the care of a specific territory within the diocese.

Section 2 of "Christus Dominus" says that bishops have the threefold duty of teaching, sanctifying, and ruling their flocks. To be able to do this, the shepherd must know his sheep; but in the huge dioceses inherited from the Middle Ages this is impossible. Large dioceses, and these are the majority, need to be broken up. In the Roman Catholic Church this is now beginning to be done. In England the Roman diocese of Southwark has recently been divided in two, the severed portion forming the new diocese of Arundel and Brighton. But the units are still too large and could well be divided again. The division of other dioceses is expected; but changes of this kind involve many problems and take time to effect. The institution of episcopal vicars offers a temporary solution.

An Anglican historian has rightly said that "If, as we believe, the apostolic episcopate in its essense is part of [the] Gospel, we shall be well advised to put it before men in its starkest simplicity, not clothed in the garments of Caesar, still less redolent of the abuses which come from power and fortuitous prestige."[8]

In the christianised Roman Empire bishops, originally simple "overseers" of local churches, were granted secular titles and insignia, and special privileges such as those reserved to the emperor or high imperial officials. These included the use of a throne at liturgical functions. Until a year or so ago ministers and servers in the sanctuary had to genuflect to the bishop seated on his throne when they approached him or passed before him: the same gesture of reverence that was prescribed when passing before the reserved Sacrament. In the eleventh century bishops assumed a special head-dress, the mitre, and from the seventeenth century they styled themselves Right Reverend. A medieval bishop, for all his dignity, was simply the Reverend Father in God *N.* or *M.* Certain bishoprics even carried with them princely or palatine rank; in England, Durham, where the last bishop to rank as Count Palatine, William van Mildert, died in 1836.

Bishops of the feudal type are still with us, but they mostly lack sufficient income to be able to make any great show of splendour outside the sanctuary. Their motor-cars are small and cheap, and do not display armorial bearings. In a few years this type of bishop will be as extinct as the dodo; with his passing an element of pageantry and colour in the church's life will have vanished.

Do bishops, priests, and deacons represent three distinct orders of ministry, or are they three grades of one and the same order? This has long been debated in the Western Church; today it is generally agreed that there is only one sacrament of holy order, but that it admits to three grades. The idea that the episcopate was a separate order to that of the priesthood was based partly on the belief that only bishops could ordain to the priesthood; but this can no longer be maintained. There is a small but definite amount of evidence to show that in the Early Church ordinations to the priesthood were sometimes carried out by clerics other than bishops. For instance St Jerome (*Ep*. 146) says that until the middle of the third century the Bishop of Alexandria was elected and consecrated by the presbyters of the city. More recently it has been discovered that during the Middle Ages certain abbots—in England the Abbot of Wigmore, for one—were granted papal indults enabling them to ordain priests for their own monasteries.

The meaning and pattern of the Church's ministry is today very much an open question, and is a field for investigation and experiment, even among Roman Catholics, who might have been thought to have settled the matter finally long ago. But now that the "Protestant" doctrine of the priesthood of the laity—which happens also to be a scriptural doctrine—has been recovered by Catholics there is bound to be deeper reflection on the part of theologians as to just what is meant by priesthood in the Christian church.

"Lumen Gentium", Vatican II's Constitution on the Church, says that since "The supreme and eternal Priest, Jesus Christ, wills to continue his witness and serve through the laity also", he "gives them a share in his priestly function of offering spiritual worship for the glory of God and the salvation of men" (section 34). Catholic liturgists emphasise that the laity exercise their priesthood most especially when they come together in church or elsewhere to celebrate the eucharist. This idea is brought out in the Mass itself at the Offertory, when the celebrant says to the people: "Pray, brethren, that my sacrifice and yours may be acceptable to God the Father Almighty".

But could a layman under any circumstances not only "offer" the eucharist, but effect its consecration? Luther, in his *Appeal to the German Nobility*,[9] said:

> . . . if a little company of pious Christian laymen were taken prisoners and carried away to a desert, and had not among them

a priest ordained by a bishop, and were there to agree to elect one of them . . . and were to order him to baptize, to celebrate the mass, to absolve, and to preach, this man would as truly be a priest as if all the bishops and all the popes had consecrated him. That is why, in cases of necessity, every man can baptize and absolve, which would not be possible if we were not all priests.

Certainly during the second, third, and fourth centuries deacons sometimes celebrated the eucharist. This was forbidden by the Synod of Arles in 314, and also by the Council of Nicaea; but there is a strong presumption that if deacons are radically able to say Mass, then laymen may be. Presumably the deacons who said Mass in the Early Church had at least tacit permission to do so; when this permission was withdrawn any such future acts would have become gravely illicit, and possibly invalid.

"Lay confession" (i.e. the absolution of sins confessed to him given by someone not in holy orders) had an even longer tradition behind it. St Albert the Great and St Thomas Aquinas held that such confessions, if made in an emergency, with no priest available, were sacramental and obligatory.[10]

When some years ago Archbishop William Temple suggested the possibility, in certain circumstances, of laymen being able to celebrate the eucharist, there was a great outcry and in some High Church quarters he was virtually accused of heresy. But Temple was a skilled theologian, as was Luther too, come to that; both of them were well versed in Scripture and the Fathers, and in traditional school divinity. It seems probable, or at least possible, that laymen (women being included in this term) do possess radically, since they share through their baptism in the priesthood of Christ, all the powers of the ordained priesthood, but may not ordinarily use them without proper commission from the Church.

When they come across such ideas as these, many older Catholics are disturbed, and are afraid that their Church is being "Protestantised"; the same cry is raised against many of the recent changes in the Church's liturgy, which are certainly open to objection, but not precisely on this ground. Protestantism and Roman Catholicism are two aspects or facets of one and the same thing, modern Western Christianity. For long hostile to one another, they are now able to see that each incorporates values which the other has lost. The recovery by Catholics from Protestants, and by Protestants from Catholics, of things of which they have been deprived is wholly good. Catholics have rediscovered the priesthood of the laity, together with the Bible and the ministry of the Word; Protestants have been able to enrich and deepen their sacramental theology and their liturgical worship. In many other ways besides there has been mutual gain as a result of the new ecumenical climate.

Protestants were not at first thought of as being "outside" the Church, but rather as a dissident element within it. Erasmus thought of Luther as a Catholic of extreme reforming views; Protestant representatives were present at the Council of Trent. The Anglican bishops were invited to attend, but were forbidden by their church's Supreme Governor, the Queen. It was not always easy at the Council of Trent to tell what was orthodox doctrine and what was not. The Cardinal of Mantua, Ercole Gonzaga, for one, was making a valiant effort to distinguish between what was of the essence of the Catholic faith and what was not when he said: "I am a Catholic. If I am not a member of the Rosary Confraternity, then have patience—it is enough for me to belong to the brotherhood of Christ."

It was a tragedy that the affair of Luther should have been so badly mishandled by the Church authorities. Few Catholics of the time had the objectivity and fairmindedness of Erasmus, who pointed out that Luther's enemies "had condemned as heretical statements in Luther's books which are regarded as orthodox and even edifying in the works of Bernard and Augustine."[11]

Another of the "Catholic" elements in church order that Protestants may be expected to recover is episcopacy as the norm of church government. This was one of the basic factors in the recent negotiations for the reunion of the Methodist Church with the Church of England, which have received a set-back for the moment because the proposed and theologically ambiguous service of reconciliation produced a high level of dissent in the Convocations of Canterbury and York. The bishop's rôle in the economy of the Church is clear. He is the official representative of Christ in the area over which he has charge; standing in the line of succession from the Apostles he is the guardian of apostolic tradition; he is the shepherd and overseer of the flock committed to him; he is its instructor and leader in the ways of holiness, and he is the celebrant *par excellence* of the eucharist.

The rôle of the priest today is much less clear. As the result of recent changes and new ways of thinking many priests are now confused and uncertain about their function in the Church and in the world. Younger priests feel themselves to be imprisoned in an authoritarian system which cripples their initiative; they feel that they are the tools of a vast centralised bureaucracy, to the detriment of their pastoral work; and they find that many things formerly done by the priesthood are now being done, and perhaps done more effectively, by others. On many of the pastoral clergy the discipline of celibacy, embraced in the enthusiasm and inexperience of youth, weighs heavily. Priests are leaving the ministry in unprecedented numbers in a state of disillusionment and in the belief that they can bear a more effective Christian witness in other callings.

What is the authentic idea of the Christian priesthood? Our English word "priest" comes from the Greek word *presbuteros*, meaning an elder. Later, the word came also to mean a leader or president of any kind of community.

The Greek *presbuteros* became in Latin *presbyter*; but somehow the meaning given to the word presbyter in Latin and in languages derived from Latin was not that of elder. Instead, it acquired the same signification as the Greek word *hiereus*, which has the same meaning as the Latin *sacerdos*, one who performs sacred, and especially sacrificial, rites: in other words, a specifically *cultic* figure. *Sacerdos* and *hiereus* both mean *priest* in the specific sense of one whose function it is *to offer sacrifice*.

In New Testament Greek the word *hiereus* is never used to denote an official of the Christian church. It is used only of the Aaronic priesthood of the Jews, and of Gentile cultic figures such as the priest of Jupiter mentioned in Acts xiv, 13.

But the term *arch-hiereus*, high priest, is applied constantly to

Christ in the Epistle to the Hebrews: e.g. in Hebrews v, 10, where Christ is said to be a "high priest according to the order of Melchizedek", a quotation from Psalm cix, 4.

Jesus, however, nowhere describes himself as a priest; nor does he speak of the Apostles as priests. But some of his sayings show clearly that he was himself conscious of a sacrificial rôle, as in St Mark's account of the Last Supper (Mark xiv, 22–24): "And as they were eating, he took bread, and when he had blessed he brake it, and gave to them and said: Take ye, this is my body. And he took a cup, and when he had given thanks he gave it to them: and they all drank of it. And he said unto them, This is my blood of the covenant, which is shed for many."

St Luke's account (xxii, 19–20) is even more clearly sacrificial. Here, after the blessing of the bread, Christ says: "This is my body, which is given for you"; and after the blessing of the wine: "This cup is the new covenant in my blood, even that which is poured out for you."

These words of Jesus can be discerned behind the thought and language of St Paul when he says of Christ in Hebrews ii, 17: "Wherefore it behoved him in all things to be made like unto his brethren, that he might be a merciful and faithful high priest in things pertaining to God, to make propitiation for the sins of the people."

The writer of the Epistle to the Hebrews makes it plain that Christ's priesthood is not that of the Aaronic priesthood, but resembles that of Melchizedek. ("And Melchizedek king of Salem brought forth bread and wine: and he was priest of God most high": Genesis xv, 18). He makes it clear that the old, Aaronic priesthood is done away with, because Jesus is "the surety of a better covenant". The old, daily sacrifices in the Temple are abrogated because Christ has now sacrificed himself "once for all". "Christ having become a high priest of the good things to come . . . entered in once for all into the holy place, having obtained eternal redemption" (Hebrews ix, 11–12). And in chapter x: ". . . we have been sanctified through the offering of the body of Jesus once for all. . . . For by one offering he hath made perfect for ever them that are sanctified."

The Last Supper took place on the evening before the first Good Friday, the day on which Jesus was to die. It seems not to have been the Passover meal (though St John, who says it was not, differs here from the three other Gospels). It was in any case a meal of a familiar Jewish type, following the traditional pattern for meals held by private groups of friends or fellow-members of small associations of one kind or another. It followed the standard pattern of such fellowship-meals, which included the blessing and distribution of bread and wine by the president of the assembly. On this occasion the familiar actions were accompanied by something new, namely Christ's words identifying the bread and wine which he had hallowed with his own body and blood "given" for those who received them, and for "many" others; and also his injunction to those who were present to "Do this in memory of me".

None of the disciples, nor, later, St Paul, would have taken the command "Do this in memory of me" to refer simply to the rite of the blessing of the bread and wine, and nothing more, for they would in any case, in the normal course of events, do this often, as a matter of course, in the future. This was the obligatory pattern for meals of this kind, and they would attend many more. No, there is something completely new here, and this new factor is indicated by the words "in memory of me", or, better, "for the re-calling of me". This familiar Jewish custom is thereby given, for Christ's followers, a completely new signification.

With regard to the command "Do this for the recalling of me", Gregory Dix says that "we have to take account of the clear understanding then general in a largely Greek-speaking church of the word *anamnesis* as meaning a re-calling or 're-presenting' of a thing in such a way that it is not so much regarded as 'absent' as itself *presently operative* by its effects."[12]

Christ's "symbolic" identification of the bread and the wine at the Supper with his own body and blood that would be offered on Calvary the next day, together with his injunction of *anamnesis*, underlie Catholic belief in the "real presence" of the Lord in the eucharistic mystery. In the past this doctrine has suffered much from the attempts of rationalising theologians to "explain" it, and these attempts have been the cause of bitter divisions among Christians. Many of these attempted explanations have long been set aside, and there is now developing a fundamental eucharistic theology which is capable of combining all that is true in both Catholic and Protestant eucharistic interpretation.[13]

The eucharistic rite is at once a re-presentation of the Last Supper and of the Sacrifice of Calvary, with which it is mystically yet really identified. According to St Paul there is only one full and sufficient sacrifice, acceptable to God, and that is the sacrificial death of Christ. Since Christ's death all sacrifices of the old Jewish law are abrogated, and all priesthood except that of Christ himself. The Last Supper was a sacrificial rite as well as fellowship-meal, and the eucharist is a sacrificial rite also; but they add nothing to the sacrifice of Calvary. Like the Last Supper, the eucharist is another *mode* of the one Sacrifice, "only the manner of offering being different" as the Council of Trent says.

Much misunderstanding has arisen between Protestants and Catholics because of the unsatisfactory thinking of certain Catholic theologians in the past about the nature of sacrifice. The Catholic Church has not approved one theory of sacrifice in preference to any other, but in the Middle Ages some very crude ideas were in circulation, some of which have lingered on until recently.

The Mass is said to be a sacrifice in so far as it is mystically yet really identical with the sacrifice of Calvary, and because the two-fold consecration, of bread and wine, is a "representative" likeness of the death of Christ. In the Canon of the Mass the rite is described as a "sacrifice of praise", which it is also.

In their *Responsio* to Pope Leo XIII's bull "Apostolicae Curae" affirming the nullity from a Catholic standpoint of the holy orders conferred in the Church of England, the Anglican archbishops affirmed a doctrine of eucharistic sacrifice which seems quite sufficient for Catholic orthodoxy. They say, with reference to the teaching of the Council of Trent, that the chief function of the priesthood is to offer the eucharistic sacrifice:

> . . . we answer that we provide with the greatest reverence for the consecration of the Holy Eucharist, and entrust it only to

ordained priests, and to no other ministers of the Church. We also truly teach the sacrifice of the Eucharist, and we do not believe it to be "a bare commemoration" of the sacrifice of the Cross—a belief which seems to be imputed to us in a quotation from that council [i.e. of Trent]. However, we think it enough, in the liturgy which we use in celebrating the Holy Eucharist—while lifting up our hearts to the Lord, and then straightway consecrating the gifts already offered that they may become for us the body and blood of our Lord Jesus Christ—to signify in this way the sacrifice which is made at this point. We observe, that is, a perpetual memory of the precious death of Christ, who is himself our advocate with the Father, and the propitiation for our sins, according to his instruction, until his second coming. For, in the first place, we offer a "sacrifice of praise and thanksgiving", then we set forth and reproduce before the Father the sacrifice of the Cross, and through this sacrifice we obtain remission of sins and all other benefits of the Lord's passion for "all the whole Church"; finally, we offer the sacrifice of ourselves to the Creator of all things, a sacrifice which we have already signified by the oblations of his creatures. This whole action, in which the people has of necessity to take its part with the priest, we are accustomed to call the Eucharistic Sacrifice. . . . But since it ought to be treated with extreme reverence, and to be regarded as a bond of Christian charity, not as an occasion for subtle disputations, precise definitions of the manner of the sacrifice, and of the principle by which the sacrifice of the eternal Priest is united with the sacrifice of the Church (which in some way are certainly one), these are in our judgement to be avoided rather than encouraged.

Roman Catholics have emphasised the sacrificial aspect of the eucharist so heavily as to practically limit their idea of priesthood to that of *hiereus*, a word, as we have seen, never used by the New Testament writers in connexion with the Christian church's ministry. Hence the Roman Catholic emphasis on the priesthood as a "sacrificing priesthood", an expression open to misunderstanding, and which has played its part in the denial by Catholics of the validity of other episcopally-ordained ministries which do not give the same emphasis to this aspect of priesthood.

What makes a sacrifice is not, as Catholic theologians have often taught in the past, some kind of destruction, real or mystical, or both, of a victim offered to God, but "the completeness of the offerer's surrender of it and the completeness of God's acceptance of it, which together make up the reality of sacrifice". St Augustine says (*De civitate Dei* x, 6) that "A true sacrifice is any act that is done in order that we may cleave in a holy union to God . . . for though it is done or offered by man, yet a sacrifice is a thing belonging to God (*res divina*), so that the old Romans used this term also for it."

The sixteenth-century Reformers were concerned to eliminate crude and over-literal ideas of sacrifice from the theology of the eucharist. Some, of course, denied that it was a sacrifice in *any* sense, declaring it to be a "bare memorial". Today the eucharist is a joint field of study for theologians of different confessions, who are able to find a wide measure of agreement. It is no longer a matter of controversy, but a subject for common study. This would have pleased Archbishop Cranmer, who said that "Christ ordained the sacrament to move and stir all men to friendship, love, and concord, and to put away all hatred, variance, and discord, and to testify a brotherly and unfeigned love between all them that be members of Christ: but the devil, the enemy of Christ and of all his members, hath so craftily juggled herein, that of nothing riseth so much contention as of this holy sacrament."[14]

At the consecration of the eucharistic elements the priest repeats over them the Lord's words of institution, "This is my body", "This is my blood", etc. For the Western worshipper this mystically identifies *the priest* with Christ. This is quite foreign to the Eastern way of thinking about the priesthood. In the Eastern Church, when the priest pronounces the words of institution, he pronounces them not *in persona Christi*, but as a narrator of sacred history. "He refers these words in the prayer to God as being uttered by Christ, and he seeks the descent of the Holy Spirit to change the elements into the Body and Blood of Christ. At no moment of worship does the Church identify the minister with Christ. . . . The priest or bishop represents the fullness of the believing worshippers who participate in prayer and the eucharistic sacrifice. . . . In worship the priest is never considered as representing the Lord."[15] He is, of course, representing the people before God, which is why he stands with his back to them, facing east, during a great part of the eucharistic action. In the new westward position now favoured in the Roman Catholic church this symbolism is lost and the celebrant finds himself symbolically facing away from God (the blessed sacrament is often reserved in a tabernacle behind his back) and towards the people.

Of course, there has been gain as well as loss. The liturgical reforms now being implemented in the Western Church are meant to present the people with a fuller, richer, and truer understanding of the eucharistic mystery and its rite. The priest is no longer a remote, hieratic figure, far away at an altar at the east end of the church. The altar is now recognisably a communion table, placed, ironically, as Cranmer directed, at the foot of the sanctuary, or even in the chancel, with the priest facing the people across it. The priest presides over the assembly of the Christian community, instructs them, and leads them in their corporate worship. It is often very badly and ineffectually done, since the priests have not been trained for this way of worship, and many dislike it. The language of the English version of the sacred texts is of a distressing banality, which does not make things easier.

The priest is now seen as the president of the eucharistic assembly; a position which is his in virtue of his position as a presbyter, the elder brother—not necessarily in years, needless to say—of the community of believers in the place to which he is appointed. His task is to make of the amorphous mass of his people a living, recognisable, and effective cell of the mystical body of Christ, his church.

This is a magnificent programme, and it is a tragedy that priests should be leaving the Church just at the time when they are being given the opportunity to realise their vocation with a new fullness. The work of the Christian priesthood has always been to administer the sacraments, to preach the word of God, and to preside over the flock. The priest who is uncertain of his vocation must still start from here; this is the basis of it all. The problem, of course, is *how* to do these things, for many of the old ways are no longer effective or relevant.

In the Catholic tradition there are seven sacraments; that is, seven sacred ritual signs which are a means of grace to those who use them rightly: Baptism, Confirmation, Holy Eucharist, Penance, Matrimony, Holy Order, and the Anointing of the Sick. Article XXV of the Church of England says that "There are two Sacraments ordained of Christ our Lord in the Gospel, that is to say Baptism, and the Supper of the Lord. Those five commonly called Sacraments . . . are not to be counted Sacraments of the Gospel. . . ." In practice, the Anglican communion recognises all seven sacraments, though not all are in equally frequent use.

Baptism, the initiatory rite which admits to the Christian church, and the Holy Eucharist, the Sacrament of the Lord's Supper, come directly from Christ in a way that the other five do not. Their symbolism is very clear, and their elements, water for baptism, bread and wine for holy communion, cannot be changed since the Church cannot alter what the Lord has specifically ordained. Not all of the other five rites, as we have them today, are equally effective in their symbolism. Some of them have been set, centuries ago, in a framework of additional prayers and ritual which have now become an obstacle to the understanding of the meaning of the rites. They are now in process of revision, and these reforms will help the priest as much as the people, for nothing is more discouraging for a minister of religion than having to perform rites which have largely lost their meaning and intelligibility.

Most baptisms in the Catholic Church, as in the Church of England, which already has a new baptismal rite, are baptisms of infants. The Catholic rite of baptism is complicated by a series of anointings and exorcisms, at least one of which is an embarrassment to perform. This is in part because the form of baptism for infants was originally one composed for the baptism of adults. No wonder that it contains many incongruities. The new rite that is being provided will correct these faults, and will also instruct the adults who are present, many of whom are likely not to be church-goers, and so may be only hazily aware of what is going on.

For many centuries one of the priest's main duties has been the administration of the Sacrament of Penance; that is, hearing confessions and imparting absolution. Although priests will normally hear confessions at any time, two or three hours are regularly given to this on Saturday evenings and on the eves of holy days. There is usually a period of confessions in the morning as well.

"Whose sins ye shall forgive, they are forgiven." Christ's commission to his Apostles is clear. There is nothing in the Gospels to say that Christ intended this power to be passed on by the Apostles to others; the Church can only have known this from the teaching of the Apostles themselves. (In the same way the Western Church, and in a large sense, it would seem the Eastern too, believes that the continuance of St Peter's primacy in the bishops of Rome is part of the apostolic tradition which the Church has received.)

In the early Roman church penitents made their confessions publicly at the beginning of Lent, and were absolved publicly on Holy Saturday. (The old and the infirm who were burdened with sins made their confessions privately.) In time, private confessions became the general rule, and in the Latin church it was made obligatory for all who were conscious of grave sin to go to confession before making their communion. Frequent—that is monthly or even weekly—confession is a fairly recent development. Since such frequent confession must normally be a matter of peccadilloes rather than of sins in the proper sense, there can be no doubt that a certain formalism has crept into the making and hearing of confessions, which has come to be hedged about with a multiplicity of legalistic regulations, most of them affecting the confessor rather than the penitent.

All the sacraments are meant to be therapeutic, spiritually effective. The long experience of the Church confirms the truth of the saying that confession is good for the soul; but the frequent confession of "venial sins", which the Church does not require to be confessed, does not seem always to produce the effects that it ought to. These confessions of devotion, as they are called, are undoubtedly a help to some; in others they seems to induce a state of spiritual self-distrust and lack of confidence that is not at all the same as the Christian virtue of humility. The stipulation of the Code of Canon Law that clerics and monks and nuns should go to confession at least once a week seems particularly unrealistic, and many nuns find the practice a burden.

The practice of frequent confession has other drawbacks; in urban parishes it makes for long queues of penitents who have to be absolved rapidly, so that those who wish for the priest's guidance on some personal problem hesitate to ask him about it for fear of taking up too much of his time and keeping the others waiting.

Through the use of "confessional boxes" the sacrament has become depersonalised. The conversation is conducted more or less in whispers through a grating, and priest and penitent are often invisible to one another. To confess one's sins kneeling down in a cubby-hole often no larger than a broom-and-mop cupboard is no help either.

A first step towards making penance once again a really living and recognisably "human" sacramental rite would be to abolish confessionals, and for priests to be allowed as a normal thing to hear confessions in any suitable place, even out of doors in fine weather.

At the present time the practice of frequent confession is falling off. Fewer people are going regularly to confession, because of dissatisfaction with the way this sacrament is administered.

Many Catholics, including priests, favour a return to some form of public penitential discipline, with private confession reserved for those who prefer it and occasions when its need is genuinely felt. In some churches experiments are being made with different forms of penitential service. These include the singing of appropriate hymns or psalms, readings from suitable passages of scripture, and a short address by a priest on the mercy of God, and an exhortation to conversion, change of heart.

Many people feel that the penances awarded by the priest before he gives absolution are now almost meaningless ("Say three Hail

Marys and one Our Father"). If a priest knew his people well and had their confidence he might say at the conclusion of a penitential service, "For our penance, next Saturday afternoon all of us who can will visit some poor or sick person and see what we can do to help them. If any of you don't know any such people, call at the presbytery and I'll fix you up."

If actual public confession of sin were felt too difficult, either absolution could be given to each one privately, after private confession, or there seems no reason why a General Absolution should not be given, without confession, as is habitually done with soldiers on the battlefield and in other emergencies. After all, Christ laid down no particular rite for the sacrament of penance, and the Church can make her own arrangements in the matter.

The priest is meant to be the friend and counsellor of his people. There is no commoner complaint about the clergy than that so few of them seem to give their people any words of advice and encouragement when they come to confession. This is hardly ever because of the lack of will to do so; in big parishes lack of time is the normal reason. But one suspects that the life of many priests today is so remote from that of their people that sometimes they do not know how to help them with their problems, other than those for which ready-made solutions are provided in the text-books of moral theology.

After the celebration of the eucharist and hearing confessions, the priest's principal task is that of preaching the Word of God. The standard of preaching today is low; but so it was in the Middle Ages. Dull, and even foolish, sermons are common. Yet the preachers are men who have received an elaborate clerical training, and are doing their best. One must remember that there is nothing more difficult, except for those who are saints, than to speak about God and the things of God.

The text of innumerable medieval sermons is extant. Most of them are of an intolerable tedium and artificiality; but perhaps they are no worse than the average modern sermon. It is impossible for us to enter into the mind of a medieval Christian, and for all one knows many of these sermons may have been highly appreciated by those who heard them.

Coming to a later age, it is impossible not to sympathise with the sentiments attributed to the Jansenist Pasquier Quesnel (1634–1719) which were condemned by Pope Clement XI in the Constitution "Unigenitus Dei Filius". The ninety-fifth of a hundred or so propositions attributed to Quesnel and selected for condemnation says that "The truths of religion are propounded to many Christians as though in a foreign tongue, and the style of preaching employed is virtually an unknown language (*veluti idioma incognitum*). It is altogether remote from the simplicity of the Apostles, and above the general level of the faithful's understanding. It is not sufficiently appreciated that this deficiency is one of the most obvious signs of senility in the Church."[16]

Complaints about bad sermons have probably always been common. But consider some of the difficulties that every preacher experiences.

First, he is faced with an audience whose levels of intelligence and education vary widely, and which probably includes children as well as adults.

Secondly, in many churches, particularly in Catholic churches, his audience will be too large for him to be able to address it in a familiar and personal way. A class of forty children in a school is recognised to be much too big; a preacher may have to speak to a hundred or more people.

Thirdly, as every teacher should know by now, to seat children in rows in front of someone who speaks to them from an elevated, superior position, is about the worst way that could be devised for teaching them. Much the same is true with respect to adults. It places an invisible barrier between the teacher and those whom he is addressing, and marks him off as a separate kind of being, a *teacher*: not one of ourselves who happens at the moment to be doing a particular job, teaching. Instead, he becomes someone *in authority*; not in the sense that he has mastered certain branches of learning, but in the sense that he has acquired a *power-relation* towards his hearers.

The passivity of the congregation is another difficulty. They must sit there in front of the preacher until he has finished; and it is not much easier for most adults to sit still and pay attention than it is for children. The natural result is day-dreaming and mind-wandering. One of the best ways to interest and hold an audience is to amuse them. Why is it that so few jokes are heard from the pulpit?

In schools these things are beginning to be understood. "Sit still" is "out"; movement, involvement, experiment are "in". The basic principle is that teachers are *persons* first and teachers second. The good teacher also knows that he is going to learn from his pupils, that he and they are exploring reality together.

Also, there must be something wrong with a system of instruction in which all the teaching is done by men. Priests are at last becoming conscious of a need to be on their guard when dealing with moral questions which affect women, and to be careful not to dogmatise about problems which occur in situations of which they themselves have no experience.

Now that the priesthood of the laity is acknowledged it seems wrong that the ordained priest should retain a monopoly of the pulpit—and if lay *men* are to be admitted as preachers, why not women? There seem to be no theological reasons of any weight to debar women from ordination if this is thought desirable. The deaconesses of the Early Church certainly received the sacrament of order, but in the society of those times the limited ministry of the deaconess would have been about as much as would have been tolerated. In the fourteenth century there was actually a lady bishop at Fucecchio, in Italy, and this lasted for a considerable time. Admittedly this *episcopessa* was not in holy orders and so could not fulfil sacramental functions; but she possessed full ordinary jurisdiction in the diocese confided to her. Dr Moorman, in his *A History of the Franciscan Order*, says that this unusual bishopric was not suppressed until well into the seventeenth century.

New and more effective ways of giving instruction in religion must be found. For instance, the old monologue sermon could alternate with a freer, simpler, way of preaching that would allow for "dialogue". Allowing the preacher five or ten minutes to set out his theme, interventions from members of the congregation could follow, and then a short period for discussion. The president of the assembly, whether the preacher himself or another, would regulate the discussion, keep it within its time-limit, and sum up at the end.

Among the younger educated Catholic laity especially there is now a good deal of bitterness and disillusionment about what goes on in church—I have even heard complaints of "Machiavellian" teaching from the pulpit—and many have given up going to Mass altogether. The "leakage" problem has been with the Catholic church in this country for a long time; what is new in the situation today is that it is the *educated* younger Catholics who are lapsing in increasing numbers. Having lost all confidence in the bishops and clergy of the "official" church, these radically-minded younger Catholics tend to make a "do-it-yourself" religion of their own based on a blend of Jungian psychology and Asian religion, with a substratum of Christianity; but there are also signs that we are going to see the emergence *within* the Catholic church of small groups or communities existing independently of any relationship with the Church's hierarchy and official structures.

It is certain that an inner, sacramental church subsists under the outward forms and structure of historic Catholicism; there is also, as we have seen from the evidence of scripture and history, reason to doubt whether the normal bishop-priest-deacon ministry is the *only* form of church order that is admissible. Experiments of this kind ought therefore to be viewed sympathetically, and not condemned out of hand by the hierarchy.

Since the schism with the East, where the proper autonomy of local churches has always been recognised, Latin Catholics have become accustomed to thinking of the Church primarily as a vast, universal, centralised body. The idea of the church as the *local* church, which is logically and actually prior to the universal or catholic church, has been lost sight of. But this was the order of thought among the first Christians. Viewed "eucharistically" the Church is present, whole and entire, mystically and yet really, in this particular assembly of Christians in this particular place here and now, prescinding from all the other communities which go to make up the Church universal.

If the local church is not allowed its proper autonomy and

dignity, a true sense of Christian community cannot begin to develop. It cannot do so as long as the bishop of the diocese regards the local churches as his personal fiefs, whose pastors can be changed at any time by his simple fiat, and which can be taxed by the bishop for his own purposes, such as the building of schools and the liquidation of diocesan debts.

As long as bishops are expected to be the administrators of vast financial enterprises, which will almost certainly be nearly bankrupt owing to clerical mismanagement, this state of affairs is likely to continue. Happily, a new kind of bishop, pastorally-minded and able and willing to delegate business administration to others, is beginning to emerge.

One of the things most needed in the Catholic church at present is a new method for the appointment of bishops. At the moment, bishops are not elected by anyone, but are imposed by the Pope. It is true that the cathedral chapter of a vacant see submits to Rome a list of three names, in order of preference, and that the other bishops of the province submit a similar list of their own choosing; but these recommendations are almost invariably ignored by the Roman authorities. This system is really no better than that prevailing in the Church of England, where the cathedral chapter holds a sham election, at which it is legally bound to nominate the person named in the sovereign's *congé d'élire*. In 1847 the Dean of Hereford, Dr Merewether, made a long and spirited protest in the chapter house after the reading of the royal *congé d'élire* naming Dr Hampden, whose orthodoxy was suspect, to the bishopric. By this courageous act Dean Merewether exposed himself to all the penalties of the statute of *praemunire*; so far his example has found no imitators, which is to be regretted.

What is needed is a system whereby both the clergy and people of a diocese may have an effective say in the choice of their pastor. The Church in Wales and the Scots Episcopal Church both have methods of synodical consultation which lead up to the final election by the governing body. The Vatican is now under heavy pressure to revise the procedure for the appointment of bishops. In a very small diocese in South America all the priests except four have recently resigned and sought posts elsewhere rather than accept the Pope's nominee, a notorious reactionary. Reform ought to be able to be achieved without resort to such extreme measures as this.

Bishops form the "ordinary" ministry of the Church; but because there are so few of them they need the presbyterate as coadjutors. But the numbers of the priesthood are now declining sharply. In Holland, where the usual number of priests at work is nearly 8,000, nearly 1,000 have left the ministry since 1964. One diocese alone has about 150 "ex-priests". The number of priests giving up is said to be increasing rapidly.[17] In 1968 189 secular and regular priests left the ministry, 50 more than the number of priests ordained in the same year. The number of men being ordained year by year has fallen from 373 in 1959 to 139 in 1968.

The corresponding figures for France have been kept secret by the bishops. This in itself is a bad sign. No figures are available for Italy; a few years ago a survey was made of 100 Italian priests who were known as "progressives". Of these 20 were found to have left the ministry.

In Brazil nearly 700 priests have left the ministry in the past three years.

In England and Wales again it is hard to get exact figures; but at least 30 priests seem to have dropped out in the last twelve months. The true figure is probably a good deal higher. And in almost all countries, Ireland included, there is a drastic falling off in the number of recruits to the ministry. In England, as in other countries, the diocesan clergy are unable to meet their commitments without help from the regular, or monastic, clergy, whose numbers are decreasing also.

In the major seminaries of Spain there were 8,087 students for the priesthood in 1955–56 and only 6,666 in 1967–68. In the last five years the ordination figures have dropped from nearly 700 to 501. These figures are for the secular clergy; in the religious orders between 1963 and 1967 the number of ordinations dropped from 669 to 501.

In Canada 158 priests were ordained in 1965 and 91 in 1968.

In the United States in the three years 1965–1968 the number of clerical students dropped from 48,046 to 33,990. Also in the

United States, 480 priests resigned from the active ministry in 1967, and 463 in the first nine months of 1968. (At the time of writing later figures are not available.)

In 1969 the Church of England, which faces a similar problem, approved plans for the recruiting and training of a part-time ministry. The Catholic church has made no move in this direction as yet; nor, in this country, is there any sign of the permanent diaconate, not bound to celibacy, authorised by Vatican II. There can be no doubt at all that a major factor in the falling off of recruits to the priesthood is the obligation of clerical celibacy; but it does not follow that the abolition of celibacy would by itself solve the problem.

In the Early Church the priesthood was not a separate caste, with distinctive clothing and a segregated way of living. Presbyters supported themselves by working in ordinary trades and professions, like everyone else, and were free to marry if they wished. At the Council of Nicaea a proposal to compel priests to separate from their wives was rejected. In the Eastern churches, both Catholic and Orthodox, it has always been the custom that priests and deacons are free to marry before ordination, but not after. Oriental bishops are unmarried, and for this reason are usually monks. In the year 386 Pope Siricius ordered celibacy for "priests and levites" of the Latin church. The instruction was widely ignored, and Pope Leo the Great a hundred years later ordered married members of the higher clergy to live with their wives "as brother and sister". Can there ever have been a more unrealistic demand? A solution was sometimes found when a wife was willing to enter a monastery. Clerical concubinage became a standing plague, and was particularly rife in the tenth and fifteenth centuries; it is said to be quite normal in Latin America today, which is perhaps why it was reported in May 1969 that in Brazil 80 per cent of the clergy had expressed themselves in favour of the abolition of compulsory celibacy.

The ideal of an unmarried clergy totally at the service of Christ and the Church is a noble one, and over the centuries it has inspired immense devotion in those capable of rising to it. But priesthood and celibacy have no necessary connexion; consecrated celibacy is a monastic idea, not a clerical one. Whether we approve or regret it, compulsory clerical celibacy is a thing of the past, and it can only be a matter of time before it is abrogated.

Much is now being written on this subject, and I do not intend to argue the matter here. The action of the Dutch bishops, who have recently approved a non-eucharistic ministry for priests who marry and wish to continue in their vocation, is a first step in the right direction. The Dutch bishops have repeatedly urged the Pope to review the question, and their action in so doing is symptomatic of the unease which Catholics everywhere are now feeling about the celibate priesthood. Even among the Italian clergy there is unrest.

Herder Correspondence for September 1969 quotes the following figures, from Vatican sources, for secular priests requesting dispensations from celibacy in 1968.

Italy	63
France	116
Spain	125
Germany, Austria, Switzerland, Holland	136
England, Scotland, Ireland	39 (a rise from 19 in 1967)
North America	230 (a rise from 89 in 1967)
Latin America	158

In 1963 the figures for Germany, etc., were 3, North America 8, Latin America 29. (Those for the other countries are not known.)

Some figures for "regular" clergy seeking dispensations from celibacy in 1968—quoted from official sources in *Herder Correspondence* for October 1969—are as follows:

Jesuits	129
Dominicans	74 (59 in 1967)
Franciscans (OFM)	146
Benedictines	55
Other Orders	714 (523 in 1967)

During the period January 1–March 20 1969, 675 secular priests requested dispensations, as against 1,026 in the whole of 1968.

These figures take no account, obviously, of priests who retired and married without going through the delays and embarrassments of the official procedures. (*Herder Correspondence* makes the comment that "The simplest way through the bureaucratic jungle is to get married first and then have things straightened out by the Roman authorities".) In any case, the lengthy questionnaire which the former Holy Office directs to be put to priests seeking these dispensations is so embarrassing in the information it demands that many feel unable to answer it.

If, however, a dispensation is sought and is granted, the Holy Office directs that the marriage of such priests must take place secretly, without witnesses, and must be recorded in a secret register. As a writer in *Herder Correspondence* says: "... the attitude seems to be that if you can't stop it happening, you might as well pretend it didn't happen."

All these tortuous bureaucratic procedures should be abrogated, since they cause nothing but suffering and scandal.

At the Roman Synod of Bishops in October 1969 the question of clerical celibacy and that of birth control were not allowed to be placed on the agenda, in spite of the urgent desire of certain bishops and cardinals that they should be discussed. At a closing ceremony at St Mary Major's basilica on October 25th the Pope went out of his way to introduce the subject of celibacy and reaffirm it as "a tremendous and sublime commitment", thereby placing it once again on a "mystical" basis which makes rational discussion impossible. Invoking the Blessed Virgin the Pope said: "Make us understand the paradoxical essence of this state." Yet earlier on the same day the Archbishops of Paris and Vienna, both of them members of the college of cardinals, had requested the Pope to ensure that the question of clerical celibacy should be discussed at the next meeting of the Synod.

In 1969 two bishops resigned in order to marry, and a former prelate of the Pope's own household received an indult reducing him to the lay state in order that he might do the same. There is something painful about these happenings, and there can be no doubt that many Catholics have been scandalised by them; but they are symptomatic of a state of affairs that cannot continue. Change will have to come.

The anonymously written article "A priest's plea for the abolition of the law of celibacy" which appeared in *The Times* of December 14th 1968 is unanswerable in terms of reason. The replies to it which were published in *The Times* and in the Catholic press attempted to dismiss it because of its "emotionalism"; but it is unreasonable to accuse of emotionalism a man who feels himself trapped in a desperate situation from which there is no way out.

It is not only celibacy itself that can be criticised—many Catholic priests would not dream of going back on their choice, and a proportion of the Anglican clergy is celibate by preference—but also the system of clerical training. It does now seem indefensible that young men of twenty-three or slightly under, who have been carefully segregated from the world, and especially from contact with members of the opposite sex, since, possibly, the age of twelve or less, should be allowed or required to commit themselves to a vow of lifelong celibacy. This is now fairly widely realised by the Church authorities, and the old seminary system of education is being modified. But the only real solution is to leave celibacy as an option for those priests who feel called to it.

To say this is not to deny the very real values inherent in the idea of celibate priesthood, and which have been developed by Pope Paul VI in his encyclical "Sacerdotalis Coelibatus". But it does seem that these values are not properly realised under a system of *compulsory* celibacy. The celibate priest bears witness in a special way to the element of *sacrifice* which should be present in the life of every priest; this is something that is in danger of being lost in the present emphasis on the priest as presbyter, and because of the current and sometimes exaggerated emphasis on the eucharist as a sacred fellowship-meal, in contrast to the former, and also sometimes excessive, emphasis on the eucharist as a sacrifice.

A change of discipline in this matter implies no rejection of the value of celibacy if freely assumed as part of the priest's life. It will be preserved specifically in the Church's religious orders; and among the diocesan clergy, as with those of the Church of England, it may be expected that there will always be a proportion of men who feel called to celibacy as a means of greater devotion to their ministry. Celibacy undoubtedly confers an "accidental" perfection on the life of the priest who feels himself called to it; but this involves no criticism of married clergy. The popes have always said that the married priesthood of the Eastern Churches is to be held in the greatest respect. As St Augustine puts it, speaking of other matters: "Alius sic, alius sic ibat."

The other remedy for the drastic decline in vocations to the priesthood is the creation of a part-time ministry. This will consist of approved men, married or single, earning their living in the normal way, who will complete in their spare time a specially planned short course of training for the ministry, and then be ordained.

There is no reason why in towns almost every small area, street, or block, which has at least a modest number of Catholics living there, should not have its own presbyter. The parish priest, at the church, under whose direction the part-time ministers would work, might well be in bishop's orders, but would be more like a rural dean than the feudal-type bishop we have been used to.

With so many presbyters available a return could be made to the kind of house-worship that the early Christians had in Jerusalem (Acts ii, 46), which would help to solve overcrowding problems in churches and obviate the necessity to spend money on building new churches. Even now, in certain places, priests are beginning to say Mass in the houses or flats of their parishioners, and usually a good number of friends and neighbours come into take part. After all, the eucharist was originally a sacred fellowship-meal, very unlike the elaborate and splendid functions of the Brompton Oratory or St Peter's Basilica in Rome.

The Church of Rome is now suffering a period of liturgical chaos which far exceeds that which has for so long been prevalent in the Church of England. The ruthless and brutal treatment accorded to the historic Mass of the Western rite on the pretext of introducing needed reforms, and the piecemeal way in which the changes have been introduced, have disturbed the faithful everywhere. Worship in the parish church being the painful experience that it now is, a "free" celebration of the eucharist might come to many Catholics as a relief.

The pattern for a "free" celebration of the eucharist would be something like this.

A small table is set in the living room of the house or apartment and covered with a white cloth. On it are placed two lighted candles in candlesticks. The table is placed so that the people present are faced by the celebrant, who stands behind it. The people can be grouped in a semi-circle if that is convenient; but there should be no one behind the celebrant. Also on the table will be a chalice, and, in a suitable dish, a sufficient quantity of household bread of good quality, brown rather than white.

The celebrant wears no vestments, and for preference ordinary civilian clothes rather than the formal clerical attire of black suit, roman collar, etc.

No altar-missal is required; the celebrant may use a small English people's missal if he wishes.

During the opening Liturgy of the Word (the Mass of the Catechumens) there will be two readings, possibly three. They need not be taken from the missal, but may be selected from the Bible or other appropriate sources, and should be selected, if possible, with a view to expressing a continuous theme. Normally the first reading will be from the Old Testament and the second from the New. If there is to be a third it may be taken from any suitable source, such as the writings of Christian mystics, the sacred writings of other religions, or from the writings of contemporary or near-contemporary Christians, such as Camillo Torres, Eric Gill, Thomas Merton, and Dorothy Day.

Each reading is given by a different reader; the celebrant may himself read the Gospel if he wishes. In any case, the readers, who may be men, women, or children, should be warned beforehand of what they are to read, so that they can look it over.

At the beginning of the Mass the General Confession is said by all together, priest and people, and the priest gives the absolution for himself and the people together. Between the Confession and the Absolution there is a short pause for silent examination of conscience. At a point indicated by the celebrant anyone who is moved to do so may publicly acknowledge some sin or failure in love of which they may have recently been guilty.

After the Absolution there is no introit-verse, since this is meant to be sung or said as the clergy enter a church in procession.

The priest, standing centrally before the communion table, leads the people in the "Lord, have mercy" dialogue ("Kyrie eleison"), and then says with them the hymn "Glory be to God on high". He then reads the collect for the day from the missal, or substitutes an extempore prayer if that seems more appropriate.

Then the first lesson is read, and this is followed at once by the Gospel reading, with the usual versicles and responses before and after.

Two or three minutes are allowed for silent meditation on the reading's theme, after which any who may like to say a few words by way of comment are free to do so. If anyone has not understood something in the reading, he or she may say so, and the difficulty may be briefly discussed. But if there is to be a homily, the celebrant may prefer to remit discussion of what has been read until after the Mass is finished.

The homily, if there is one, should be short, and carefully prepared. Anyone who wishes to ask a question during the homily, or to add some comment, is free to do so.

Then the Creed is said if it is a Sunday or a major festival. The third reading, if there is one, may then take place, while the celebrant is busy with the Offertory rite.

At the Offertory—the offering to God the Father of the bread and wine to be later consecrated—the priest takes in his left hand the dish holding the bread, and in his right hand the chalice—which he has just prepared with wine and water—and elevates them to a foot or so above the table while he says the Offertory prayer.

Then follows the "Orate, fratres" ("Pray brethren") dialogue, after which the "Sanctus" ("Holy, holy, holy") is said by all. The priest then reads the appropriate Preface, or he may extemporise a Preface of his own.

For the Canon of the Mass, which now follows, the celebrant may use any of the four Canons now authorised, or he may extemporise his own Canon, with prayers for the special needs of the group or community present, and its members.

At the remembrance of the living the celebrant will name aloud those whom he wishes specially to remember, and other names may be added by any of those present.

At the twofold consecration the institution narrative is said by the celebrant in the usual way. Since the celebrant is facing the people, the elevations of the consecrated elements are omitted.

At the remembrance of the dead, the same procedure as at the remembrance of the living.

The Our Father is said by all together, as is the "Agnus Dei" ("Lamb of God, who takest away the sins of the world . . .")

Either before or after he makes his communion the celebrant divides the consecrated bread into a sufficient number of portions for those who are going to communicate. Then he distributes the bread, each person taking a portion in his hand and communicating himself. All then drink from the chalice, which the celebrant administers to each severally.

After the communion the priest cleanses the chalice, reads (or says extempore) the final prayers, and dismisses the assembly with his blessing.

To celebrate a eucharist of this kind will at first be more demanding for a priest than the formal rite to which he is used. There the priest is, properly and intentionally, impersonalised by the vestments which he wears and by the formality of the ritual. Here he is bound by only the minimum of liturgical convention, and must show himself to be in truth the "elder" who presides in love at the assembly of Christ's friends. In his extempore prayer especially he must be seen and heard to be sincerely involved in this meeting of his fellow-Christians; the same sincerity and commitment must be able to be sensed in his homily.

No priest who has celebrated, or even been present at, a eucharist of this kind will be troubled with doubts and hesitations over his place and function in the Church and in the world. His function is to lead the Christian people, and others if he can, to

holiness: to union with God and with one another through love;
to lead them, not as one who is holier than they are, and above
them, but as one of their own number who has been chosen to
serve them in this special way.[18]

FIVE

MONASTICISM

THERE have been monks and nuns in the Christian church from very early times, and they form an important "estate" in both the Catholic and the Orthodox churches. However, monasticism cannot be said to be an essential element in the Church, for it was not established by Christ; but those who follow this way of life appeal to certain sayings of Christ's for its justification, and as sanction for the three vows of poverty, celibacy, and obedience. Present-day religious,[1] in spite of their firm discipline and cloistral existence, have been much affected by the prevailing state of uncertainty and unrest in the Church, and many have begun to question the validity of their vocation in the modern world. Some have come to despair of it in its present form and have returned to the world to take up other vocations in which they see the possibility of a more effective Christian witness and service. Among these are senior men: abbots, provincials, and priors. In most orders there is considerable unrest among the younger members. In 1968 ninety-two student-friars of an Italian province of the Franciscan Order left in a body, in protest against the authoritarian and paternalistic way in which the affairs of their province were conducted. In the United States recently all the members of a large community of teaching nuns returned to civilian life in order to be free as teachers from the interferences of male clerical control.

In the United States something like 11,000 members of religious orders opted out in 1968.

Long before the present crisis most religious orders were experiencing a shortage of recruits. There was an upsurge of vocations after the last war, but it had spent itself at least ten years ago, since when there has been a progressive decline. For a while this was attributed to the materialism of the age, but this is now seen to be an insufficient explanation. The Christian community which is a religious order will always have many of the same problems as the larger community, the Church, of which it is part, and unless the religious orders can replace with something better the outworn structures and authoritarian ways of thinking and acting that characterise them, the dearth of recruits will continue, since they now have little to offer that appeals to young men and women with a burning desire to work with others for the creation of a better world.

In England, as in other countries, if things go on as at present it will not be long before the monastic scene is much the same as it was at the end of the Middle Ages, when large abbeys and priories were more than half empty, inhabited by a few ageing and discouraged religious striving ineffectually to keep up the traditional observances. Already there are signs that this will be so. The English Dominicans, the order by far the most aware of the needs of the times, have been forced by declining numbers to give up the church and priory built for them by André Raffalovich at Pendleton, Manchester, early in the present century. Their novitiate has been moved from the beautiful priory of the Annunciation at Woodchester, in Gloucestershire, and merged with another community, leaving the priory with a ghost community of four. The Dominican student-friars have been removed from Hawkesyard Priory in Staffordshire, where a reduced community occupies one-half of the great building, the other having been turned into a retreat house and conference centre for public use. The Dominicans have closed their two schools, one of which had had a long and distinguished history since it was founded in the Low Countries during the reign of Charles II by the Dominican cardinal Philip Thomas Howard.

With the other orders it is much the same story of dwindling or empty novitiates and the departure of student-religious before they reach ordination. One order in the space of twelve months recently lost eight priests. Even the Society of Jesus, for long the largest and most flourishing order in the country, is in difficulties and has had to close its famous public school at Beaumont, Old Windsor.

When one realises that only one-third of any group of novices reaches the priesthood, the implications for the future are black. Some of the secular clergy openly voice their satisfaction at this state of affairs, and say that in a few years' time all priests will be secular priests. This is a very short-sighted attitude, since even now the seculars are so short of men that in many places they cannot carry on without the help of the regulars, and it is an illusion to think that young men who feel drawn to monastic life are likely to substitute for it the life of the diocesan clergy.

In many Roman Catholic parishes numbers of people would have to go without Mass on Sunday if the parish priest could not rely at weekends on the assistance of some neighbouring religious house. On a Sunday morning there may well be three Masses in the parish church, and one in the evening. In addition there may be a hospital or prison to be served, as well as one or more "Mass centres" in outlying parts of the parish. Few parishes, unless they happen to be in the care of a religious order, will have enough priests to cope with all this.

So monks and friars leave their monasteries on Sunday morning, or even on Saturday evening, to give the help needed, with the result, all too often, that their own churches and their own community life suffer. The Divine Office is not becomingly celebrated, for lack of numbers, and a High Mass, or even a Sung Mass, is not possible, except in the larger houses, for the same reason. The sacrifice is in a good cause, no doubt; but the price paid is a considerable impoverishment in the quality of conventual life.

In considering the state of the religious orders today some questions asked by George Gordon Coulton, one of the greatest modern medievalists, are relevant. In the opening pages of the first volume of his *Five Centuries of Religion*[2] Coulton says:

The Religious Orders have been among the main forces of European civilization; at certain times and in certain places they may perhaps have been the greatest of all civilizing forces. Yet every government in Europe gradually followed Henry VIII's example, and herein the State seems to express the mind of the individual, since adult vocations to the cloister are now extremely rare, among men at least. . . .

Even in the Middle Ages, Religious must sometimes have doubted not only of final perseverance (as they constantly confess) but also, to some extent, even of wisdom in their choice. They must have asked not only: "Need I give up so much?" but even: "Is it right to look upon the abandonment of some of these things as a sacrifice to God?" . . .

The root problem of monasticism is one which every ideal has to face. . . . Can we best serve our higher aim by crystallizing it into a society within Society, and so cutting ourselves off from the contagion of the unideal multitude? Or is it a braver and more effectual choice to keep full touch with the rest, . . . hoping gradually to leaven the world by constant intercourse?

These are important questions. But we can hardly hope to be able to answer them unless we are agreed on the fundamental purpose of the monastic life, bearing in mind, however, that the external forms in which it is embodied are capable both of diversity and of development. The monks of medieval Europe lived a life very different from that of the fourth-century monks of the Egyptian Thebaid; and a medieval religious would be greatly astonished by certain aspects of monastic life in the twentieth century.

It is generally understood that the monk leads a life apart from that of society, and that this life is thought of as being in a special way dedicated to the service of God. But most people, Catholics included, are not clear as to what this implies. If they view monks and nuns favourably it is usually on account of their visible achievements; for their work as scholars, educators, builders, agriculturists, and so on, and also perhaps for the splendour of their public worship.

These reasons for esteem, though valid in their degree, are really beside the point, for they have nothing to do with the fundamental purpose of monastic life.

For a short, sound exposition of the meaning of monasticism we cannot do better than go to the classic work of the seventeenth-century English Benedictine Augustine Baker, *Sancta Sophia*, or *Holy Wisdom*. In section three of the First Treatise of his book[3] Father Baker says:

> What is it, therefore, that a soul truly called by God to enter into religion [i.e. the "religious" life] looks for? Surely not corporal labours; nor the use of the sacraments; nor hearing of sermons, &c. For all these she might have enjoyed perhaps more plentifully in the world. It is, therefore, only the union of the spirit with God by recollected, constant prayer; to the attaining which divine end all things practised in religion do dispose, and to which alone so great impediments are found in the world.
>
> The best general proof, therefore, of a good call to religion is a love to prayer. . . .
>
> It is a state, therefore, of recollectedness and introversion that everyone entering into religion is to aspire unto, which consists in an habitual disposition of soul, whereby she transcends all creatures and their images, which thereby come to have little or no dominion over her, so that she remains apt for immediate co-operation with God, receiving His inspirations, and by a return, and, as it were, a reflux, tending to Him, and operating to His glory.

A little further on Father Baker says:

> . . . by the Rule of our holy Father St Benedict, all his disciples are obliged to propose to themselves no other end of their religious profession but only such purity of soul and the operations of it in spiritual prayer; so that how exact soever they be in outward observances, unless they be referred unto, and efficacious also for the producing of, this internal purity, they shall not be esteemed by God to have complied with their vocation and profession.

Father Baker supports this doctrine with two quotations from the fourth to fifth century monk John Cassian: (a) "The end of a monastical profession and the supreme degree of all perfection consists in the perfection of prayer"; (b) "This is the end of all perfection, that the mind becomes so purified from all carnal defilement that it may be raised up daily to spiritual things, till its whole enjoyment and every motion of the heart may become one uninterrupted prayer."

This is the doctrine common to the traditions of monks and nuns of both the Western and Eastern churches. And it is as applicable to canons regular and to friars as it is to members of the monastic order in the stricter sense. For in their convents canons and friars lead a life of full monastic observance, though a great deal of their work may lie elsewhere. St Dominic always carried with him on the journeys that took him half over Europe a copy of Cassian's *Collationes*.

Monastic life, then, within its framework of community life and regular observance, is a life directed specifically towards attaining union with God through intensive prayer. In the Holy Rule St Benedict speaks of the monastery as "a school of the Lord's service", and directs that those who seek to enter are to be carefully scrutinised in order that it may be seen whether or no they are "truly seeking God" and are fervent in prayer.

In other words, the monastic life is essentially a *contemplative life*.

The same is the teaching of the first Carmelite writing known to us, a late thirteenth century work known as *The Book of the First Monks*, which summarises the traditions of the hermits on Mount Carmel before their migration to Europe. The anonymous writer says: "This life has a twofold end. The first end we reach with the help of grace by our own labour and our continual striving towards virtue. It is: offering to God a clean and pure heart, a heart free from every stain of sin. The other end is given to us by God's liberality; viz, that not only after death, but even in this mortal life, we already experience to some degree God's presence and the joy of heaven."

The Venerable John of St Samson, a sixteenth-century Carmelite laybrother, known as "the blind mystic of Rennes", expounds the same doctrine. "He who strives", he says, "towards this contemplation with all his bodily and psychic powers, and so lives according to his vocation, as far as it is possible, is in some sense holy enough. And if he does not get very far into this extensive region, let him do what he can."

At this point a possible misunderstanding needs to be removed. From what has been said so far it might seem that the monk's is a self-centred life. But this is not so. He lives in a community precisely in order to avoid the dangers of an extreme individualism; and he undertakes his work of self-reformation in order that he may become progressively less self-centred, and more and more God-centred. The God-centred man sees all other beings somewhat as God sees them, that is with an intensive love and sympathy. The monk's life is a life *for others*, even if it is lived apart, as it will be even within his own community, where there will be times and places of silence, and where his cell is supposed to be a kind of spiritual fortress, free from invasion.

So in the end the monk will be judged on the extent to which he has become a man of prayer, a man of God; not on his success or otherwise as a preacher, scholar, writer, artist, teacher, or administrator.

The monk should be living in the presence of God all the time; but he cannot actually be at prayer all the time. There is work that must be done, and the monastery is supposed to be self-supporting as far as possible. He has to earn his keep as far as he can. So it is important to know what kind of work is suitable for monks and what is not.

St Benedict says in his Rule (ch. xlviii) that "Idleness is an enemy to the soul; and hence at certain times the brethren ought to occupy themselves in the labour of their hands, and at other times in holy reading. . . . And if the needs of the place, or their poverty, oblige them to labour themselves at gathering in the crops, let them not be saddened thereat; because then they are truly monks when they live by the labour of their hands, as did our fathers and the Apostles." St Albert of Vercelli who in his Rule for the hermits on Mount Carmel directs that they shall remain in or near their dwellings, meditating on the law of the

Lord, unless other just occasions prevent them, devotes a whole chapter to "Assiduity in Work, for the Avoidance of Idleness".

From the first, manual labour had an important place in the life of the monks of the West. Some of their time was taken up, as St Benedict directed, by the *opus Dei*, the daily round of common prayer. At first the chanting of the psalms and hymns of the Divine Office was a quite short and simple matter; but long before the end of the Middle Ages it had developed into a cycle of lengthy and elaborate church services, with a splendid panoply of ritual. This took up several hours of the day, and manual labour began to be left to unordained brethren. For by that time most of the monks were in holy orders.

The monastic life had gradually become clericalised, and for priest-monks manual labour was replaced by literary and scholarly pursuits. This came about largely through the indirect influence of the canons regular. In chapter lxii of the Rule, "Of the Priests of the Monastery", St Benedict says: "If any Abbot desire to have a priest or deacon ordained for his monastery, let him choose from among his monks one who is worthy to fulfil the priestly office." He warns such priests not to "become forgetful of the obedience and discipline of the Rule", but to "advance ever more and more in godliness", keeping always the place due to them, and not claiming any precedence because of their priesthood.

The early monks were nearly all laymen; the canons regular, by contrast, were a specifically clerical body. About the year 360 St Eusebius, Bishop of Vercelli, had formed the clergy of his cathedral church into a college or community leading a common life, with profession of celibacy and obedience, in accordance with a Rule drawn up by himself as superior. This canonical way of life, so called from the Greek word *kanon*, meaning a rule, was regarded as in some way related to the common life of the first Christians in Jerusalem. Eventually bodies of clergy other than those attached to cathedrals began to live according to this pattern, and from them eventually developed the various houses and congregations of canons regular.

St Augustine of Hippo had organised his own clergy in this way. Eventually the so-called Rule of St Augustine, a conflation of two letters written for the guidance of a community of women presided over by his sister, superseded the rules written by Albert of Vercelli, Chrodegang of Metz, and others, and those who followed it became known as Canons Regular of St Augustine, or Austin Canons.

The canon regular is always either a priest or a candidate for the priesthood. In his abbey or priory he leads a full monastic life, which he combines with the carrying out of the daily church services with as much solemnity as possible. He is also expected, if required, to undertake the cure of souls, so that canons regular often take charge of parishes, which may be situated at considerable distances from their monasteries.

The monastic and canonical orders interacted on each other. The canons, previously governed by provosts in the larger houses, took over from the monks the office of abbot; and the monks turned their abbots, originally laymen, into prelates lacking little of the outward splendour of bishops. By the end of the Middle Ages almost all monks were priests, except for novices and students, and uneducated "lay brothers" were introduced to take care of the manual work. Conversely, certain houses of canons gave up the cure of souls and lived lives of almost Carthusian enclosure and seclusion.

Manual work having been more or less abandoned among the Black monks,[4] it was to a large extent replaced by literary and scholarly pursuits, and by teaching. This was held to be justified by St Benedict's directions about holy reading, although he clearly envisaged a balanced régime of prayer, manual work, and study. On grounds of health alone this was desirable; and in fact the discipline of manual labour has never quite disappeared even from the more sophisticated kind of Benedictine house. David Knowles records in his memoir of Abbot Cuthbert Butler[5] that during part of the time that he was Abbot of Downside Dom Butler was "in the habit of digging in the garden for an hour or so on two or three days in the week; the spectacle was then to be seen of the abbot president of the English Benedictine Congregation, who was also a scholar of European reputation, issuing from the door of his abbey carrying a spade over his shoulder, rifle fashion, and wearing mud-encrusted boots, ancient trousers and tail coat green with age, with a shapeless green cap on his head, worn back to front." "It says much", Dr Knowles continues, "for the mental power and distinction that was present in every line of Abbot Butler's countenance that even when so clad he would never have passed for an ordinary man."

It is Professor Knowles's opinion[6] that it was precisely the lack of satisfying occupation that was one of the greatest difficulties in the monasteries of the late fifteenth century. Agriculture and the manual crafts had come to be considered unsuitable occupations for priests, so that the copying and illuminating of books became the usual employment for priest-monks. But by the middle of the thirteenth century the religious no longer had a virtual monopoly of these clerkly skills, and had to face outside competition. By the end of the fifteenth century these occupations had become "fossilised and artificial", and no longer gave their practitioners a sense of creative achievement. By that time in any case the invention of printing had arrived to supplant them.

In some places, as with the great Maurist Benedictine congregation in France, works of pure scholarship became the typical monastic activity. Something of this tradition is still to be found in some English houses of Black monks, notably at Downside, Ampleforth and Nashdom (the latter being in communion with the see of Canterbury); but since the Order's post-Reformation revival the typical activities of English Benedictines have been teaching and parish work. St Benedict expected there to be some boys in the monastery, who would become future monks, and he directed that their faults should be corrected by "severe fasting or sharp stripes". These boys were educated in the monastery, so that teaching has a long history as an occupation for monks. Whether it can be held to justify the management of large fee-paying public schools, with five or six hundred boys and a considerable lay staff, is another question; but certainly not a few monks seem to find satisfaction in it.

It seems unlikely, however, that this kind of school can survive much longer under our modern social and educational systems. Economics alone will probably kill them, for with the number of monks being likely to continue to decline, the financial burden of having to employ an ever-increasing number of lay masters will probably become intolerable.

Part of the explanation of the current exodus from religious orders, and their failure in recruitment, may be the fact that these institutions, like their medieval predecessors, are no longer able to offer their members satisfying occupations. In many houses there is now not even an adequate liturgy to support the contemplative life. For the monk, canon, or friar in the past, whatever the trials and difficulties of his life might be, always had the support of the choir. The daily singing of the familiar sacred texts to the familiar ancient plainsong was a constant source of spiritual inspiration and strength which raised his soul to higher things and brought him near to God. Now the Latin liturgy, which has been in a sense the backbone of the monastic life for nearly fifteen hundred years, has been summarily thrown out, and all that is offered in its stead is a sorry mess of pottage, a mish-mash of Knoxian and sub-Knoxian texts,[7] to be sung, if at all, to the wan melodies of Gelineau and the insipidities of composers of "People's Masses".

It is quite true that monastic life is cluttered up with a whole lumber of outworn and irrelevant practices and conventions, but to lay rude hands on the most venerable usages just because they are old, and not "with it" in the view of philistine reformers, is the way not to repair the crumbling structure of monastic life, but to bring it down in ruins.

One of the justifications for monasteries and convents must surely be that they house communities where the Christian life is lived intensively, by men and women wholly dedicated to the service of God through service to the wider community of which they are part. "Service" and "Community" are ideas that have great appeal to the young today; but generally speaking they find them more effectively realised elsewhere than in the Church's religious orders.

Community life today in many religious houses is more like life in a fairly cosy bachelors' club than it is to the common life of the early Christians, with one heart and one mind in God. But this is nothing new. It was Coulton's judgement, based on his extensive knowledge of the period, and it is Professor Knowles's judgement, confirmed by actual experience of monastic life over many years, that the life of the medieval monasteries, for all its saints and its achievements, fell very far short of an adequate realisation of the monastic ideal. The Orders had too much wealth, too many members, and too many houses. Many monks and nuns had taken to the life as a respectable occupation, and with too little concern for the things of the spirit. Abbots and priors were immersed in secular offices and ranked as feudal lords. If the religious were idle it was because there was nothing of interest for them to do, hence their frequent recourse to hunting and hawking. The obligations of the common life were widely evaded on one pretext or another, largely by means of a system of privileged exemptions. The whole system was worn out, probably beyond the possibility of revival, before Henry VIII put an end to it for his own far from disinterested reasons.

How do things stand today, one hundred and seventy-three years after the beginning of the monastic revival in 1796, when French Cistercians, exiles from the Revolution, founded St Susan's monastery at Lulworth?

Some Orders still have too many members for spiritual health; many have an excess of external commitments—schools, parishes, etc.—which have often been unwisely assumed in order to win the favour of local bishops. This has led in some instances to a lowering of the standards of recruitment in a desperate attempt to keep the numbers up. Then there are too many men in the Orders who have entered as an easy way to the priesthood rather than out of any devotion to the monastic life for its own sake. Superiors today are not engaged in secular employments, but they are sometimes unduly attached to office. In Orders where the superiors are not elected but are appointed by some form of governing body, a kind of "old boy network" sees to it that when their terms of office expire they are simply translated to new positions of authority, a process which is liable to continue until old age sets in, or beyond. The common life is reasonably well kept; but the notion that the religious lead a life of "holy poverty", except in an academic sense of the term, has worn pretty thin. It is doubtful if any religious order in England today could be described as wealthy; some are even in debt. But Chaucer and Langland would recognise in some modern religious superiors the old unhealthy interest in legacies and benefactions which they satirised. All *ad majorem Dei gloriam*, no doubt, but open to misinterpretation.

Where renewal and adaptation are concerned the monks have a considerable advantage over the friars, and over most canons regular. Within a loose federation each house of monks is an autonomous unit, or is destined to become so if it is not already. Within the wide limits of the Rule each community is free to determine its own way of life and its own kinds of work and apostolic activity. Friars have no such advantage. All the houses in each province are subject to a common higher superior, the Prior or Minister Provincial. The provinces in turn are dependent on the General of the Order in Rome and his Council. Consequently, every alteration and improvement in the way of life has to be fought for over long years before it can take effect. The outlook for such unwieldy and highly centralised bodies as the friars is not hopeful. The canons regular are mostly in the same position. With a few exceptions their houses are now grouped into congregations, each of which has an Abbot General in Rome or elsewhere. The plight in this country of the senior canonical body, the premier religious order of the Western Church, the Canons Regular of the Lateran, is critical. Their abbey at Bodmin, one of the most attractive religious foundations in Great Britain, now houses only a tiny community, and there are no novices.

It is fairly generally realised now among religious that community life as most of them have experienced it is not what it should be. All too often there is little real sense of fraternity; the gap between St Augustine's apostolic ideal of *Cor unum et anima una in Deo* and the reality is too great. Voltaire is supposed to have said that religious "are people who come together without knowing each other, live together without loving each other, and die without regretting each other". Things are rarely as bad as that; but the fact is, that while a religious ought to experience a good deal of solitude, his existence ought not to be one of *loneliness*, and it is to be feared that the life of many religious in their communities is fundamentally a lonely life, and that this loneliness has in the past accounted for many defections.

A report issued in May 1969 of a discussion held by the Carmelite friars of the Province of Rio de Janeiro states that it was agreed by those taking part that the main cause why so many religious do not arrive at a fully human development as persons must be attributed to the fact that in their training the centre of gravity was that of chastity rather than love. It was candidly admitted that some members of the Province had given up and left, without at the time having any intention of marrying. But often a woman came along and filled the already existing emptiness, with marriage as the natural result. It is good to find Carmelites discussing the crisis of their Order with such candour and discernment; the spirit behind such discussions affords some hope for the future.

The Holy See is aware that all is not well with the orders. In January 1968 it issued an *Instruction on Renewal of Religious Formation* which seeks to open up a way for renewal by means of certain ideas which are put forward on an experimental basis since "it is evident that no clear and definite legislation can be formulated except on the basis of experiments carried out on a sufficiently large scale and over a sufficiently long period of time." The principal point which it makes, a wholly sound one, is that much greater attention must be paid to the stages in religious life previous to the taking of final vows. The age of admission to novitiates should be raised, and there must be a preliminary period of testing and formation, lasting up to two years, before candidates are admitted as novices. Except in purely contemplative orders the novitiate is no longer to be a period of absolute seclusion from normal contact with the world. Instead, there is to be "a proper balance of periods set aside for solitude with God and others devoted to various activities and to the human contacts which these involve".

The temporary vows made at the end of the novitiate, and binding for three years, may now be replaced by some form of less binding promise, made not to God but to the community. The

Instruction recognises that "a certain number of young candidates come to the end of their novitiate without having acquired the religious maturity sufficient to bind themselves immediately by religious vows, even temporarily". The purpose of this is to eliminate the perpetual stream of petitions for dispensations from temporary vows that flows into the offices of the Sacred Congregation for Religious in Rome. These are certainly wise provisions; but it is not likely that they will do much to arrest the general decline from which the orders are suffering, since, as with the priesthood, celibacy is no longer an ideal that has much attraction for the young.

The monastic way of life comes down to us from a time when the idea that celibacy was a higher state than that of marriage was universally accepted in the Christian church. The thought of St Augustine lay behind this view, and his influence still lies heavily behind Catholic teaching on sex and marriage. His treatise on *Marriage and Concupiscence* teaches that every sexual act, even within marriage, contains an element of sin. "Although", he says, "conjugal copulation for the generation of offspring is not itself a sin (because the good will of the mind controls the pleasure of the body instead of following pleasure's lead, and the human judgement is not subjected to sin), yet in the use of the generative act the wound of sin is justly present." Anyone who believed this would naturally consider celibacy to be a higher state than marriage. No one thinks in this way now, and celibacy has to be embraced, if it is, from quite different motives.

Present-day novices usually have the monastic idea of celibacy explained to them as part of the *sacrificial* aspect of the life, with particular emphasis on the monk's free surrender to God, from a supernatural motive, of one of the best things that God has given us: the possibility of marriage and the life of the family. This is a sound approach; but it no longer carries quite the conviction that it used to since, however attractive an idea in itself, it is part of a general ascetical ethos which is today being called in question.

This, of course, affects every area of Christian life, but in a special way the monastic area. As long as this world was thought of as *divinely intended* to be a vale of tears, so that the more suffering one endured in it the higher would be one's place in heaven, a high premium was obviously placed on voluntary, supererogatory sufferings. Among these, the voluntary assumption of lifelong celibacy ranked high. Today we are more likely to think of this world not as a prison to be endured for the sake of joys to come, but as a place in which we explore reality, and by so doing render ourselves progressively more capable of adaptation to another and higher order of reality to be encountered after our physical death.

This way of looking at our human life and destiny must lead to the rejection of many older attitudes, and the question may be asked: has monasticism in its traditional forms any future in a world which is no longer able to accept so many of the old monasticism's basic attitudes?

To raise these questions is not to discount the need for a sane asceticism in every human life: there is no avoiding the need for non-attachment to things and to desires if we are to lead good lives. This involves walking along that straight and narrow way which is the same as the Buddha's noble eight-fold path, consisting of right views, right intentions, right speech, right conduct, right livelihood, right effort, right mindfulness, and right concentration.

So asceticism, that is self-discipline, self-training, as part of a human life is not in question.

There is no need to stress the difficulty of the celibate ideal, which in itself is a noble one. But it is hardly a vocation to be offered to the average man, and unhappily, religious orders are full of average men and women, so that the number of failed vocations throughout the ages is no matter for surprise.

From this point of view the falling off in the number of vocations to the religious life is to be welcomed. Nothing could be more misguided than the feverish efforts now being made by many religious orders to beat up recruits by means of advertisements in newspapers, talks to children in Catholic schools, "Vocations Exhibitions", and the like. This is not to say that even very young children may not sometimes be conscious of a vocation to the priesthood or to the religious life; but this is a special grace, which many priests, monks, and nuns have experienced, without any prompting from parents, relatives, teachers, or members of the clergy.

The complaint that it is the practice of the friars to attract into their orders boys who are too young to know their own minds is a very old one.[8] It formed part of the indictment levelled against the friars, the Franciscans especially, by Richard FitzRalph, Archbishop of Armagh, in his sermon on the text "Judge not according to the appearance, but judge righteous judgements" preached at a papal consistory at Avignon on 8 November 1357. St John Capistran was once heard to say, when discussing the affairs of the Observant Franciscans with Pope Eugenius IV: "If you should wish, holy Father, to carry out a proper reform of our Order, there are three P's that you must get rid of." The three P's were *Pecunia*, *Pueri*, and *Petulantia*; that is, money, young boys, and irresponsibility in office-holders." The saint's advice is not entirely irrelevant today.

The present minimum age for admission to novitiates is sixteen. It could well be raised to twenty-five; and it would probably be a good thing if the taking of final vows were not allowed until much later than is now customary.

It is not likely that the monastic life will disappear. There will always be men and women drawn to the dedicated life of contemplation and service, whose generous dispositions find their fulfilment in the self-discipline and self-sacrifice of the vows. The pattern of life sketched out by St Benedict in his Rule has an appropriate timelessness, and is as relevant in the present century as it was in the fifth.

Probably there will be fewer monasteries in the future, and smaller ones. And while it is true that the monk and nun need for their work a definite amount of silence and solitude, which can be secured within the framework of a life in community, this does not mean that the monk or nun has to be totally cut off from the larger human community. This has been recognised in the Holy See's recent legislation for contemplative, enclosed communities of women. The unreasonableness of the nuns never being allowed out, and of speaking to visitors from behind spiked grilles and with veiled faces, while the television is installed in the community recreation room, is too evident for such anachronisms to be able to survive.

Monasteries will always be needed. Their quiet "sapiential" presence is more necessary than ever in the cold, impersonal climate of the age of technology. Probably they will tend to be more "open" than in the past. As technology advances, man's thirst for "wisdom" seems to become stronger. It springs from the human need for the direct intuition of reality, the *simplex intuitus veritatis*, foundation of all true religious experience. This is the wisdom, or gnosis, that all the major religious traditions of mankind seek to impart. But in the modern Western Church the contemplative life is hardly flourishing. Those in search of this wisdom seldom come to our monasteries; when they do, too often they do not return. Seekers after the traditional wisdom go rather to the exponents of the Hindu, Buddhist, Zen, or Sufi traditions, or to the schools claiming to impart the doctrines of such teachers as Gurdjieff or Ouspensky. Yet the Western Church has her own mystical tradition, as rich as any of these; but if it is known at all today, except to scholars, it is through old writings such as *The Cloud of Unknowing* and Walter Hilton's *The Scale of Perfection*. Some of those who frequent the schools of other traditions come to Catholicism in the end because they are able to recognise that the eternal wisdom is still present under the formalised rites and juridical structures of modern Roman Catholicism. But it is rarely Catholics who have taught them to see this.

One of the most disturbing things that present-day religious find in their life is the question of holy poverty. The religious makes public profession of discipleship to the Poor Man of Nazareth, and confirms it by vow. Yet there is nothing noticeably poor about the way he lives. It is true that he has no possessions of his own, and that all his earnings go into the common fund of the community which supports him. But he lacks for little or nothing. He is assured of a roof over his head, has a room of his own, possibly three good meals a day, and no worries as to what is going to become of him in his old age.

Another disquieting feature is the number of religious orders which have in recent years acquired mansions, or even castles, for their own purposes. True, it can be argued that if the orders did not acquire them these historic properties would probably fall into ruin; but it is an uncomfortable thought that St Dominic and St Teresa, and many others of the saints, have warned their followers against building or living in large and stately houses.

This akropolomania is like something left over from readings in Sir Walter Scott in a distant Irish childhood. It seems to have little to do with the "adjourned" Church of the 1960s, but rather to be a hangover from the restored Church of the 1820s, the Gothic Revival, and the monkish interludes of Victor Hugo's plays.

Certainly there is nothing ostentatious in the way the religious live; but it is an unmistakably *secure* life, and younger religious today are disturbed by this. For the plain fact is that the followers of holy poverty, at least in the "free" world, are a definite part of the "affluent society" and enjoy a standard of living that is not only higher than that of millions of people in the under-developed countries, but is also higher than that of the slum-dwellers in Notting Hill and Glasgow.

The decline in recruitment to the religious life is due in part to the ease, if not comfort, in which the modern religious lives. There are, of course, other factors in his life which make for considerable discomfort. The common life in which everything is prescribed and nothing is of one's own choice is an exacting discipline to surrender to; but this cannot be seen from outside, it has to be experienced from within. What can be *observed* of the way religious of the older orders live is not likely to encourage any young man or woman conscious of the miseries of Vietnam or Biafra to join them.

Of course, it is possible for the individual religious to lead an effectively poor life. Father Vincent McNabb must have saved his Order considerable sums of money by his practice of walking everywhere in London and not using public transport; also by writing his letters on the backs of printer's proofs or on the inside of the dust jackets of books, and re-using his correspondents' envelopes when sending his replies. And since he always wore his habit, he never had to have a suit of clothes made; and his habits being made of handwoven cloth lasted three or four times longer than ordinary ones.

The religious who is prepared to go to such lengths, and to cut out the use of tobacco altogether, in order to make himself feel a little of the pinch of poverty, shows a certain heroism, but he does not really accomplish much as he is still living off a system which professes poverty, but in practice negates it.

But this is nothing new. The medieval monk lived an incredibly austere life by modern standards; yet he too was materially better off than most of the people outside his monastery. The problem is perennial, and perhaps insoluble. A partial answer to it would be to stop talking about poverty and to replace it with the idea of "the common life". Canons regular have always done this. This cuts out hypocrisy, but it does not solve the problem of how to prevent communities of celibate men and women from living too far above the poverty line. Their industry, together with the generosity of the faithful, creates the problem for them; and they can hardly escape being influenced by the generally rising standard of living around them. Since the younger generation will have none of this it looks as if the days of formally ordered and elaborately structured religious orders are over.

Monasticism has had a remarkable revival over the last one hundred and fifty or so years, but it seems as if it got off to a wrong start. All over Europe, the Orders were virtually swept away after the French Revolution. This gave the little bands of survivors a magnificent opportunity to make a new beginning, a real *aggiornamento*. But no one seems to have realised that the world had changed, and that the feudal type of religious life no longer had a place in it. Far from that, the medieval monastery was regarded as the classic, all-time example to be followed, and so thanks to Dom Guéranger, who entertained a highly romantic view of monastic life in the Middle Ages, Solesmes arose somewhat on the pattern of Cluny, and the liturgical worship of the monks took on a medieval splendour. Liturgy became a spectacle, and monasteries centres of tourism. Now, all that is over, or nearly so. It seems certain that never again will monasticism occupy the dominant position in society which it had in the Middle

Ages, and for that we may be thankful. The fact of the matter is, the religious orders were already finished long before the Revolution, and when the time came for their revival, they were revived on partly mistaken lines.

The romantic, Wagnerian notion of the religious life was stimulated by the cult of the crack-pot, who seems to be almost the typical figure in the Church at times of general indifference to religion, just as the martyr is the typical figure in times of hostility and persecution, and the confessor in times when the Church is approved by society. The personality cult of eccentric near-geniuses has flourished in the monastic world during the past century or so; one has only to think of such spellbinding figures as Father Ignatius of Llanthony and Abbot Aelred Carlyle. These men, and others like them, in order to fulfil their need for self-realisation and for the monastic revival of their dreams, propagated a romantic, visionary, and folkloric brand of religion and of monasticism that had an immense appeal and brought in the funds needed for the realisation of their grandiose projects. These men were absolutely sincere, and not without a degree of holiness; unfortunately, they usually left behind them, for their less gifted successors to cope with, a collection of decaying white elephants and of financial embarrassments. In their fantastic efforts to restore the monastic life these men were in fact assuring its rapid decay.

Yet there is a great deal that is admirable in the monasteries of today. The brethren are faithful to their duties and live together surprisingly harmoniously considering their different origins and temperaments. One may sometimes perceive a cynical glint in the eyes of older brethren when the psalm *Ecce quam bonum* ("Behold how goodly and pleasant it is for brethren to dwell together in unity") is sung at receptions and professions; but by and large their experience will have borne out what the psalmist says. Sick and ageing brethren are most carefully looked after; and the occasional erring brother who has "gone off the rails" in one way or another is always treated with great understanding and indulgence. The religious are sincere, hard-working men; but with the contemplative element in their vocation falling into increasing dis-esteem, and the lack of anything creative to replace it, it is not surprising that many of them are now asking exactly where the relevance of their life is to be found. Few of them with any length of claustral experience can fail to recognise the truth, and applicability to themselves personally, of the words in which Professor Knowles has summed up the story of the pre-Reformation religious orders in England.

> At the end of this long review of monastic history [he says] a monk cannot but ask what message for himself and for his brethren the long story may carry. It is the old and simple one; only in fidelity to the Rule can a monk or a monastery find security. A Rule, given by a founder with an acknowledged fullness of spiritual wisdom, approved by the Church and tested by the experience of saints, is a safe path, and it is for the religious the only safe path. . . . When once a religious house or a religious order ceases to direct its sons to the abandonment of all that is not God, and ceases to show them the rigours of the narrow way that leads to the imitation of Christ in his love, it sinks to the level of a purely human institution, and whatever its works may be, they are the works of time and not of eternity.

"It sinks to the level of a purely human institution. . . ." This is the ever-present threat to monasticism. If monasteries cease to be schools of the Lord's service, where eternal wisdom is both taught and learned, this is what must happen.

Christianity, as has been said, is to do with people loving God and loving each other and caring about each other. That is what the life of our religious communities is about, and few who belong to such communities today are unaware that somehow their light is not shining before men as it should. It may be that community life in the traditional form will be replaced by freer, less formally organised groups, without vows, and without the corporate ownership of property. Such communities would not need to be self-perpetuating, but could be dissolved, or completely re-recruited, after so many years. The members of such communities would cultivate a deep interior life while at the same time contributing actively to the struggle against war, racial discrimination, and poverty. These groups of committed Christians, in which men and women would live and work together, might very well work in close relationship with a monastery of the older kind, whose light would thus radiate outwards in a new way.

SIX

EAST AND WEST

AT the time of the "Humanae Vitae" crisis a number of conservative English Catholics took the line that it was just a clamour raised by a few hotheads, and that in a little while everything would quieten down and everyone would recognise the rightness of the Pope's teaching. It is not likely that anyone thinks so now. Either we are witnessing the final crack-up of the Roman church, or else it is going through fires which will be the catalyst of a phoenix-like regeneration.

Curial and other vested interests are so firmly entrenched in the Latin church that it may be incapable of reform from within in a sufficiently thorough, rapid, and effective way to prevent its decline and dissolution, or absorption into some nebulous "Great Church" of the future. A really effective purification of the Latin church is not going to be brought about by a few modest reforms in the spirit of Vatican II, nor by the present Pope's sumptuary laws depriving cardinals of their hats and shortening the length of their trains.

The imbalance so deeply rooted in Latin Christianity can only be corrected through reunion with the East. In the West an urge to explain and define the inexplicable and the undefinable has produced the arid effects of a sterile scholasticism far removed from the living dialectic of Scotus and Aquinas. The Eastern mind

157

is disposed rather *not* to define than to define; to emphasise and dwell on the mystery of things rather than to provide a formally logical apologetic. St Thomas Aquinas is at one with this Eastern tradition of apophatic theology when he says in the *De veritate*: "What God actually is always remains hidden from us; and this is the highest knowledge we can have of God in this life, that we know him to be above every thought that we can think of him."

For Easterns, the Church is seen not as a juridical institution but as the sphere *par excellence* within which union with God is attainable in this present life, and within which all the conditions required for reaching union with God are available.[1] It seems that in some way God has to be *experienced* before reasoned attempts to demonstrate his existence can have any effect, yet once the divine has been experienced, "proofs" are no longer relevant. In thinking about God the *via negativa* of St Thomas and the apophatic theology of the Eastern Church express between them the mystical unity of Eastern and Western Christianity which subsists underneath outward divisions and dissensions. Eastern and Western theologians may seem at times to speak in almost different languages; but the mystics of both East and West speak in the same language because of the timeless truth of what they say. What could be more "up to date" than this passage about God and union with God from the Dialogue between a Master and his Disciple written by Robert, the fourth prior of the Austin Canons of Bridlington, about the year 1150?[2]

Master: Now let us see in what sense God is said to be in heaven. For God is not contained within spacial limits. . . . We must understand that God, who is everywhere, is in a place, yet is not localized. A thing is said to be localized when it is bounded by the regions proper to a place, above and below, before and behind, right and left. But since angels and human souls cannot be enclosed within the bounds of place, far less can that incomprehensible Being be so confined. For if we think of God's place as being in the heavens, as in the higher regions of the world, the bird's desert is greater than our own because their life is lived closer to God. But it is written, not that the

Lord is nigh unto them that dwell on mountains, but that *the Lord is nigh to them that are contrite in heart*; and that is something that pertains to lowliness.

But as the earth was called a sinner when it was said to the first Man, *Earth thou art, and unto earth thou shalt go*, so on the other hand a righteous man can be called a heaven. For it is to the righteous that the apostle says, *For the temple of God is holy, which temple ye are*. Wherefore if God dwells in his temple, it is correct to say *Who art in heaven*, who art among the saints.

This Western Christian text could easily be paralleled from Eastern sources.

Christianity is a supernatural religion, not just a code of ethics or body of reasoned beliefs. It is a supernatural religion because its doctrine is *revealed* by God, through Jesus Christ. It is also supernatural in the sense that its doctrine, if *lived*, will free a man from imprisonment in his own faulty nature and will raise him to a higher and more authentic level of existence which is his *real*, eternal life, from which somehow he has become estranged.

Thus the doctrine of the Fall, set out symbolically and "mythically" in the Book of Genesis, is at the foundation of the Christian faith.

From St Augustine onwards theologians have seen that there is something irrational about the notion of a God who creates out of pure love rational beings enjoying union with himself, the source of all goodness and happiness, who deliberately turn away from their Maker in search of lesser goods. Such a situation seems to be strictly inconceivable.

Even more unsatisfactory is the idea of a God who freely chooses to create finite beings whom he foreknows will freely and culpably rebel against him and so deserve eternal punishment.

A contemporary theologian has suggested an interpretation of the Fall that seems to fit the facts of human existence, and which thus goes a long way towards dispelling these clouds of irrationality. In a recent article on "The Problem of Evil" Professor John Hick says:[3]

In creating finite persons for fellowship with himself God

has given to them the only kind of freedom that can endow them with a genuine (though relative) autonomy in relation to himself, namely cognitive freedom, the freedom to be aware or unaware of their creator. He has created them at "an epistemic distance" from himself through their emergence in a world which God has set apart from himself as a separate creaturely sphere. . . . Man's creation at an epistemic distance corresponds to what the Hebrew myth of the beginning calls his fallenness. That is to say, man was not brought into existence in the direct presence of God and with an unclouded awareness of his maker."

Hence, as St Thomas Aquinas teaches, the existence of God is not self-evident.

This view or interpretation of the doctrine of the Fall does not minimise the reality of the presence of evil in the world, but it avoids the necessity of assigning to Satan the rôle of a kind of anti-God whom God has to placate by the sacrifice of his Son. (Inadequate interpretations of the Fall lead to inadequate interpretations of the Atonement.) "Our actual human situation", Dr Hick says, "with all its ambiguities, is not the work of the Evil One seeking to thwart God's will, but represents a phase in the outworking of God's intention."[4]

The *fact* that man is in some way estranged from his true Centre, and "very far gone from original righteousness", is evident; or at least evident to most men. This *condition*, which Christian theology has rather clumsily labelled "Original Sin", seems to be exactly what the Buddhist means by *avidya*, or "ignorance".

The Christian revelation teaches that man does not need, and ought not, to remain in this "fallen" condition. God makes it possible for man, through the grace won by the atoning and redeeming actions of Christ, to transcend this state of imprisoned self-centredness and to be reborn into a higher life of love and freedom, the life of "grace", unconfined by the limits of space and time, through union with Eternal Being.[5]

Christianity is a doctrine of liberation and enlightenment. "I am the light of the world," Christ says: "he that followeth me walketh not in darkness." The writer of the Fourth Gospel says of Christ: "There was the true light coming into the world, even the light which enlighteneth every man. . . . As many as received him, to them he gave the right to become children of God, even to them that believe on his name: which were born not of blood, nor of the will of the flesh, nor of the will of man, but of God."

Christians believe that man cannot by his own natural powers extricate himself from the web of illusion and the miasma of self-centredness that his "fallen" state involves him in, but that he can do so by the grace of God. This is man's proper task. Even in this mortal life he can lead a "heavenly" existence. He can attain this state, at least in some degree, through the work of self-purification by means of prayer and the sacraments. As a holy modern priest has put it: "For men of every position and of every origin there is only one way to peace: purification of the heart and the proper direction of the energies."[6] If a man does not attempt the task, but goes through life like an automaton or a sleep-walker, his last state will be worse than his first, for after death, which is the gateway to full self-realisation in God, his consciousness will remain totally unfitted for adaptation to the new condition of "eternal" life. The suffering which this must entail is the truth behind the doctrines of hell and purgatory, with whatever imagery we invest them.

This is what Jesus was saying when he spoke with Nicodemus:

> . . . the same came unto him by night, and said to him, Rabbi, we know that thou art a teacher come from God: for no man can do these signs that thou doest except God be with him. Jesus answered and said unto him, Verily, verily, I say unto thee, Except a man be born anew he cannot see the kingdom of God. Nicodemus saith unto him, How can a man be born when he is old? can he enter a second time into his mother's womb, and be born? Jesus answered, Verily, verily, I say unto thee, Except a man be born of water and the Spirit, he cannot enter into the kingdom of God. That which is born of the flesh is flesh; and that which is born of the Spirit is spirit. Marvel

not that I say unto thee, Ye must be born anew. The wind bloweth where it listeth, and thou hearest the voice thereof, but knowest not whence it cometh and whither it goeth; so is everyone that is born of the Spirit. Jesus answered and said unto him, Art thou the teacher of Israel and understandest not these things?" (John iii, 1–10)

St Gregory of Nyssa, one of the early Greek church fathers, says: "We enter into eternal life through baptism and resurrection. Baptism, an image of the death of Christ,[7] is already the beginning of our resurrection, a way out of the labyrinth of death."[8]

The Western Church, with its strong moralising tendency, has been much preoccupied with the question of how man is to settle his accounts with God; hence its doctrine of *merit*, culminating in the complex notion of indulgences.[9] The Eastern Church, by contrast, emphasises the doctrine of man's *deification*. The difference is clearly seen in the two churches' treatment of grace. For the West, grace is a transcendent but *created* quality by whose means "justification"[10] is imputed to sinful man, though not exactly in the sense that Luther used the word "imputation".[11] Lossky says:[12]

> The notion of a state of grace of which the members of the Church can be deprived, as well as the distinction between venial and mortal sin, are foreign to Eastern tradition. All sin, even the most trifling, that of the inward state of the heart no less than that of an outward act, can render our nature opaque and impenetrable to grace. Grace will remain inactive, though always present, united to the person who receives the Holy Spirit. The sacramental life—"the life in Christ"—is thus seen to be an unceasing struggle for the acquisition of that grace which must transfigure nature; a struggle in which victories alternate with falls, without man ever being deprived of the objective conditions of salvation. In Eastern spirituality "a state of grace" has no absolute or static sense. It is a dynamic shifting reality which varies according to the fluctuations of the infirmities of the human will. All members of Christ who aspire to union with God are more or less in grace: all are more or less

deprived of grace. As Ephraim the Syrian says: "the whole Church is the Church of the penitent; the whole Church is the Church of those who are perishing."

The "deification", or *theosis*, of the creature cannot, of course, be fully realised in this life, but only in the aeon to come; but even during this present life a degree of union with the divine can be attained if the creature makes full use of the means which God has made available. This transformation of our nature is symbolised in Christ's changing of the water into wine at the marriage feast at Cana, and is the meaning of Christ's words: "Every one that drinketh of this water that I shall give him shall never thirst; but the water that I shall give him shall become in him a well of water springing up unto eternal life."[13]

In their theology of the Holy Trinity there is a marked difference in the way in which East and West speak of the Holy Ghost. Western treatment of the Holy Spirit is very inadequate; so it is not surprising that there is comparatively little devotion to the Spirit in the West. The formularies of the Roman Missal show that the Church worships God the Father *through* the Son and *in* the Spirit. This is the order of things in the Canon of the Mass, and the same order is observed in the conclusion of all the collects of early date. But in later collects, as in many Roman Catholic popular devotions, prayer is often addressed to the person of Christ, in his humanity, with the Father and the Son taking second place. Where this order predominates the true theocentric character of Christian worship is weakened; and when popular devotion to the Blessed Virgin takes unbalanced forms, a further distortion of orthodox belief and worship follows.

The weakness of the Latin church's Trinitarian formulations is probably due to some extent to the limitations of Latin as a language of theological discourse, as against the greater flexibility of Greek. The Latins seem to have confused the *procession* (*processio*) of the Holy Spirit with his *mission* (*missio*), so that this confusion was one of the factors in the *Filioque* controversy which did so much to embitter relations between the two churches. The creed formulated at the Council of Nicaea and approved by the

Council of Constantinople contained the clause: "I believe in the Holy Ghost . . . who proceeds from the Father." In spite of canon 7 of the First Council of Constantinople, which said that ". . . it is not permitted to anyone to bring forth, or write, or compile any other creed than that which was determined by the Holy Fathers who met, in the Holy Spirit, in the city of the Nicaeans", the Latins amended the clause to read: "I believe in the Holy Ghost . . . who proceeds from the Father and the Son." This interpolation seems to have had its origin in Spain in the late sixth century. When it began to spread to other parts of Christendom its use was forbidden by Pope Leo III; but eventually it was adopted even in Rome.

The Eastern Church protested from the beginning against the intrusion of this formula. Eventually, at the reunion councils of Lyons and Florence the Greeks were obliged to accept the "procession" of the Holy Spirit from the Father *and* the Son, but they did not have to incorporate the *Filioque* clause in the creed. The union did not last, and the *Filioque* has remained a major theological difference between East and West.

On the Western side the matter has become less of an issue because Western theologians now tend to represent it as a battle over words rather than a basic difference in belief. Those Eastern writers who continue to emphasise the importance of the *Filioque* controversy are on surer ground.[14]

The Trinity is the central doctrine of the Christian faith. It is the greatest of all religious mysteries. Christ himself spoke of God as Father ("my Father and your Father"), of himself as the Son of the Father, and of the Holy Spirit which the Father would send to guide the Apostles and the Church after Christ's ascension. The doctrine is set out concisely in the Apostles' Creed (probably by origin an early Roman formula for the profession of faith at baptism), and was affirmed in simple outline in the Creed of Nicaea. For the removal of heterodox interpretations of the doctrine the Early Church fathers defined the relationship within the one divine essence of the Father, Son, and Holy Spirit, as a relationship between three "Persons" or *hypostases*, a technical notion taken over from Greek philosophy. The divine Persons differ only in origin. The Father is ungenerated, the Son is generated by the Father, and the Holy Spirit *proceeds* from the Father.

The more elaborate Athanasian Creed (the "Quicunque vult"), a fourth or fifth century Western profession of faith, affirms:

> . . . the Catholic faith is this: That we worship one God in Trinity, and Trinity in Unity;
>
> Neither confounding the Persons nor dividing the Substance.
>
> For there is one Person of the Father, another of the Son; and another of the Holy Ghost.
>
> But the Godhead of the Father, of the Son, and of the Holy Ghost is all one: the Glory equal, the Majesty co-eternal.
>
> So that in all things . . . the Unity in the Trinity and the Trinity in Unity is to be worshipped.

The Christian's assent to the doctrine of the Trinity is not just a matter of acceptance of a mysterious proposition; belief in the Trinity is a living influence with the believer, since it is to the Second Person, the Son, Word, or Logos, that he owes his redemption, and to the Third Person, the Holy Spirit, his sanctification. In the life of the Eastern Church the Spirit is an experienced reality in the life of the Christian in a far more conscious way than it is in the Western Church.

The Son is "generated" by the Father eternally, and the Spirit "proceeds" eternally from the Father. The Western idea that the Spirit proceeds from the Father *and* the Son leads to an attitude of mind that regards the Spirit as being *subordinate* to the Father and the Son, and this way of looking at things may well be a factor behind the idea that both the universal Church and the General Council are in a relation of total subordination to the Pope.

A recent anonymous Orthodox writer goes so far as to attribute the failure of the Council of Constance to secure acceptance of the Pope's subordination to the Council to the Conciliarists' inability to formulate their proposition satisfactorily because of a deficient theology of the Holy Spirit.[15]

It is certainly due to Orthodoxy's greater consciousness of the rôle of the Holy Spirit in man's sanctification and in the life of the

Church that Orthodox church discipline is so much more humane and Christ-like than that of the Roman church.

This may be seen especially in the Orthodox attitude to marriage. The Western Church has maintained for centuries a rigidly biological attitude towards marriage, insisting that its primary and over-riding purpose is the procreation of children, and that secondarily "it was ordained for a remedy against sin, and to avoid fornication".[16] Orthodoxy finds, as the Western Church is now beginning to find, that the meaning and purpose of marriage is present primarily in the love of husband and wife, which makes of their union an authentic replica of the love which exists between Christ and his Church.

The spirit of Orthodoxy stresses the freedom of the individual Christian and the liberty of the children of God over and against every kind of institutionalism and organisation. There is no urge for the constant definition of the indefinable purely for the sake of definition; no urge to add to the number of truths held to be "necessary for salvation". Divorce and remarriage are tolerated, under certain conditions, for the avoidance of greater evils, such as those which follow from Latin rigidity in this matter.

Nowhere does Latin legalism and rigorism cause greater suffering than in the sphere of marriage. To such an extent has this become a scandal that in October 1968 Monsignor Stephen Kelleher, the presiding judge of the matrimonial tribunal of the diocese of New York, resigned his post, which he had held for twenty-five years, in protest. In a statement he condemned the tribunals, of which he had experience both within and outside the United States, for producing delayed justice, sometimes no justice, frustration, humiliation, distrust, suspicion, and fear. He proposed that marriage tribunals should be abolished, that each person should be free to decide in his or her own conscience whether or not he is free before God from one marriage and therefore free to enter another, and that a system of marriage commissions (not courts) should be established to help individuals to reach responsible decisions in these difficult matters.[17]

In his diocesan leaflet for December 1968 the Bishop of Exeter, Dr R. C. Mortimer, chairman of the Anglican archbishops' commission on divorce, and one of the most Catholic-minded members of the episcopal bench, advocated that the Church of England should adopt the Orthodox discipline on divorce and remarriage. Interviewed by a *Times* reporter, the Bishop of Wakefield said that he welcomed the Bishop of Exeter's suggestion because "Both as bishop and parish priest I have been unhappy about the unyielding attitude of the Church in this matter, and have often found it difficult to reconcile with the love and care that the Church, as the body of Christ, must show to those in need."

When Christ said "Those whom God has joined let no man put asunder" he cannot have meant that the marriages of those who go through a church service which did not then exist are absolutely incapable of dissolution for any cause whatsoever. Everything must depend on what is meant by "Those whom God has joined". Marriage is the gift of husband and wife to each other. This mutual giving consists of much more than the physical union alone. The complete giving of the one to the other involves spiritual, psychic, and emotional reciprocities, as well as the physical, which in some instances prove absolutely incapable of realisation. When this is so in an overwhelming and irremediable degree, there is no marriage except in a legal sense, even though the Church has bestowed its blessing on it and the State has registered it.

Such "marriages" should be recognised as null from the simple fact that they have irretrievably broken down, and the partners should be permitted, if they wish, to enter into new relationships, seriously embarked on, rather than be condemned to the loneliness of lifelong celibacy or the stigma of "living in sin". The Western Church is now involved in the hypocrisy of pretending that flagrant legalised misalliances are marriages in a sacramental sense unless some canonical and legalistic fault can be found in the manner in which the marriage was contracted. This is to place the future happiness of two human beings in the hands of the extremely fallible clergymen who administer the matrimonial tribunals, and involves the parties concerned in all the agonies of humiliating inquisitions and long-drawn-out legal processes. The whole ghastly business of so-called "nullity" suits in the diocesan and Roman church courts should be abolished outright.

To do so would involve no weakening in the *standards* of marriage which the Church upholds, only a merciful concession to the weakness of human nature.

Here is an instance, told me by one of the persons principally concerned, of the extreme fallibility of the workings of the Church's machinery for dealing with matrimonial cases.

A few years ago a Catholic layman wished to marry a lady, also a Catholic, who had been civilly divorced from her husband, who was still living, many years previously. As a Catholic, she could not lawfully contract a new marriage unless the former union could be declared canonically null.

The lady's husband was not a Catholic, so that the marriage had taken place under a dispensation granted by her bishop. This dispensation was a dispensation for what is technically known as "mixed religion"; that is, a marriage of two Christians one of whom is a Catholic and the other a member of some other Christian denomination. Everything seemed to be perfectly in order, so that later it seemed at first that there could be no possible grounds on which to petition for the marriage's annulment.

However, in the course of investigation into the circumstances of the marriage it somehow emerged that the lady's husband had never been baptised and so was not a Christian. This meant that the dispensation for the marriage was invalid, since what should have been obtained was a dispensation for "disparity of cult", that is for the marriage of a Christian with a non-Christian.

This seemed to offer grounds on which a declaration of nullity might be hoped for. A petition was presented to the matrimonial tribunal of the diocese in which the lady and her intended future husband were living, and was forwarded to the Sacred Roman Rota for the decision of the Holy See.

After a considerable delay, amounting to many months, a negative decision was given by the Rota.

All hope of the couple being able to contract a canonically valid marriage seemed at an end, when somehow the case came to the notice of the bishop of the diocese and aroused his personal interest. The petition was reworded and sent in again to the Rota, this time by the bishop himself; and in due course an affirmative answer was received, declaring the previous marriage null and void on the ground that the dispensation authorising it was invalid.

There can be no doubt at all that this was a correct decision in the circumstances; but it was only through what is perhaps best called an act of providence that it was obtained. Many petitions for annulments of broken marriages have to be refused on technicalities; others, objectively well based, as was the one here described, fail through lack of perspicacity on the part of church lawyers, as did this one in the first instance.

In its moral theology of marriage the Latin church has been excessively preoccupied with sin, and consequently with minute regulations for right and wrong behaviour which show little understanding of the "existential" aspects of marriage. The same legalistic attitude is behind the canon law which invalidates the civilly contracted marriage of a Catholic even with a non-Catholic, and makes the children of such a marriage canonically illegitimate. This seems to flout the Church's sacramental theology of marriage —which affirms that the parties themselves, and not the witnessing priest, are the ministers of the sacrament.

And in this age, when an increasing number of stable unions are established without any public form of marriage, by couples who wish to avoid entanglement with either Church or State, it is difficult to see why the Church, and society in general, cannot recognise such unions as having at least an authentic social status.

With regard to marriage in general, and the question of family limitation in particular, it would seem to be significant that Christ emphasised the *unitive* nature of marriage, but said nothing, as far as we know, about its reproductive aspects. The encyclical "Humanae Vitae", in condemning birth control as contrary to natural law, seems to have overlooked St Thomas Aquinas's dictum: "Things that are of natural law vary according to the various states and conditions of men" (*Summa Theologica*, Supplement, q. 41, a. 1, ad 3m).

There ought to be no reason why East and West should not agree on a common marriage discipline; such agreement would bring reunion of the two churches much nearer. They can only be further estranged by such incidents as the Vatican reaction to the marriage in the Orthodox church of Mrs Jacqueline Kennedy to Mr Aristotle Onassis, when Mrs Kennedy, the widow of a former head of state, was rebuked in insulting terms in an interview given to newspaper men by the prelate in charge of the Vatican press office. The Archbishop of Boston, Cardinal Richard Cushing, forthrightly came to her defence, and said: "The point I want to make is this. . . . This idea of saying she's excommunicated, she's a public sinner, what a lot of nonsense. Only God knows who is a sinner and who is not. There are so many ramifications with regard to anything that might be considered sinful that only God Almighty could really interpret them and manifest his love for the sinner, while at the same time despising the sin."

SEVEN

ECCLESIA SEMPER REFORMANDA

IT is usually difficult to pinpoint exactly the event or events that provoked a particular crisis either in Church or State. The Reformation can be conveniently traced back to Luther's Ninety-Five Theses as the fuse that lit the powder-barrel; but before Luther there were Wycliffe, Hus, and many others. However, it is convenient, and not unreasonable, to find the beginning of the present crisis of the Roman Catholic church in this country not so much in the encyclical "Humanae Vitae" as in the widely publicised defection from the Church and its ministry of the Reverend Charles Davis at Christmas 1966. Certainly it was this event that provoked the famous editorial in the Dominican review *New Blackfriars* for February 1967, which led to the dismissal and suspension of the editor, Father Herbert McCabe. The departure of Father Davis came as a great shock to Catholics, for he was well known and highly respected as a theologian, both on account of his writings and his distinguished editorship of *The Clergy Review*. The editor of *New Blackfriars* was perhaps guilty of some exaggeration when he described Father Davis as the Church's "foremost theologian" in the country; and of bias when he accused a priest who had described Davis as a "lightweight" theologian (lightweight, that is, in comparison with such men as Yves Congar and Karl Rahner) of showing "quite special theological ignorance and frivolity". But there can be no doubt that

171

for the hierarchy Father Davis's departure was a major misfortune because it aroused a storm of criticism of Church authority, and embittered the already strained relations between the educated laity, who owed a great deal to Father Davis, and the bishops.

In a widely publicised interview Charles Davis had said that "The official Church is racked by fear, insecurity and anxiety, with a consequent intolerance and lack of love." "There is concern for authority at the expense of truth, and I am constantly saddened by instances of the damage done to persons by the workings of an impersonal and unfree system." Father McCabe had commented in his editorial:

> These charges seem to me to be very well founded and their truth would, on the whole, be taken for granted by English Catholics. The Church is quite plainly corrupt: a Cardinal[1] selects Christmas as the occasion for supporting the murder of Vietnamese civilians; the Pope alleges that the Church's teaching is not in doubt about birth-control; the Congregation of Rites has just asserted (*Times* January 5th) that a family communion celebrated in a private home and followed by a meal is a practice "alien to the Catholic religion", while nearer home and more comically a Bishop[2] has expressed the fear that Catholics who sing carols in Anglican churches are endangering their faith and morals. This is the kind of thing we have come to expect of Cardinals and Popes and Bishops and Curial Congregations. . . . We have grown accustomed to seeing the Church like this; so accustomed that we are surprised when a man gives it as his reason for suddenly leaving the Church— almost as though he had seen it for the first time. We have lived with this truth so long that we have perhaps forgotten how scandalous and horrible it is: like people who live with racial discrimination and slavery.

It is only too true that we have "grown accustomed" to seeing the Church like this, so that it took the extensive newspaper and television publicity given to Charles Davis's departure to set off an agitation for reform which has since grown to such proportions that there is small possibility of its being stifled.

The message has sunk in; if the hierarchy and other religious superiors cannot alter their authoritarian methods of government they will before long find themselves with no one to govern except the ageing and dwindling "simple faithful" who are conditioned to authoritarian government and to having their consciences formed for them by the clergy. But there are signs of better things. From the first the Archbishops of Westminster, Liverpool, and Birmingham showed pastoral concern and insight in their handling of the "Humanae Vitae" crisis, and a number of other bishops followed their lead. All these bishops have taken seriously the urgent need to reform Church organisation in this country along collegial lines through the establishment of diocesan priests' senates and lay commissions. If the lower clergy and the laity respond to these initiatives, good results may be expected.

In some dioceses bishops will probably be slow to implement the needed reforms, and will seek to "immobilise" the new consultative and advisory bodies, and to render them as nugatory as possible. It is not yet certain that the laity are ready and able to discharge effectively their new responsibilities. In the 1920s and '30s, when the late Lord Rankeillour was working for the establishment of parochial church councils in Roman Catholic parishes, he got little support from the laity and his endeavours came to nothing. Similarly in the 1930s, when a grandiose national "Catholic Action" organisation was established with lay officers and a distinguished lay president, it came to nothing because of general lay apathy. So there are likely to be difficulties; but the signs are that they will be overcome.

To reform the Church by first reforming the local churches is the right way to set about it, even if it involves the risk of encouraging separatist tendencies. To reform the Roman church itself is a vastly more difficult thing, seeing that the curial and other reactionary forces are so firmly entrenched. Since its separation from the East the Latin church has developed into a rigid autocracy governed by the Supreme Pontiff, with his vast, universal, and never-to-be-questioned powers and by the elaborate and impersonal bureaucratic machinery of the Roman Congregations acting in his name. The Church, has, in fact, for centuries been governed largely by fear: fear of the Pope, with his power of dismissing cardinals and bishops at will, with no possibility of appeal; fear of the Curia and Roman Congregations on the part of bishops; fear of the bishops by the clergy; and fear of the parish priest on the part of the laity—this latter being usually "reverential" rather than "servile" fear.

The Pope is as much trapped in this system as anyone else; for the Latin church has now become quite simply too big for one man to govern—heads of modern states have the same problem, hence the many movements towards federalism and regionalism in different countries—and the larger the bureaucracy built up to help the Pope, the more unwieldy and inefficient the whole thing becomes. It has now reached a point at which the Pope has become the Prisoner of the Vatican in a quite different sense from that intended by Pius IX, or whoever it was that first coined the phrase. He is imprisoned doctrinally by the self-imposed need always to conform, or at least to appear to conform, to precedent; and he is imprisoned also in the sense that he is "protected" by his entourage, which is dominated by the conservative elements in the Vatican, from seeing many documents, and not only documents but also people, that he ought to see. In spite of aerial journeys to the Holy Land, India, South America, New York, and Africa, the pontiff is increasingly out of touch with what is going on in the local churches of his patriarchate. The bishops themselves complain of the Pope's remoteness and of the Vatican's unsatisfactory communications system. Father Bernard Häring, a moral theologian of international reputation, and a member of the Pope's birth control commission, has described how members of that commission were not allowed to see the Pope. "We had no possibility to approach the Pope. In my eyes he was walled in."[3] The new Synod of Bishops, which could have been a magnificent instrument, in union with the Pope, of collegial church government, is still a merely consultative body. The enlarged college of cardinals is largely a collection of Vatican place-men, forced, on being admitted to their dignity, to take a humiliating oath to observe total secrecy regarding the "instructions" which they may receive from the Pope. Secrecy, of course, is one of the most effective weapons of authoritarian régimes. (It is only very recently that in religious orders "subjects" have been acknowledged to have a right to be informed of what is discussed, and what decisions are reached, at meetings of superiors, and to know of the financial resources and position of the communities to which they belong.)

These attitudes are characteristic of Church authority at every level. Men who are by nature kindly and sympathetic become overbearing and ruthless when the "system", on whose maintenance their own position depends, seems to be threatened. The vicar general of the first English diocese in which priests were suspended for expressing conscientious dissent from "Humanae Vitae" said of one of these priests, "I feel terribly sorry for him, but once he is out of the parish he doesn't matter any more." As the writer of a letter to *The Guardian* observed: "Hardly a Christian precept, but one which is crucial to the working of any authoritarian power structure." The same prelate said bluntly: "The Catholic Church is autocratic", as though that disposed of the need for any further discussion. Of course, he was confused by the suddenness with which the situation had arisen; the bishop of the diocese was absent, and his second-in-command was not used to being harried by reporters and television men. In dealing personally with the incriminated priests he was kind and courteous. But kindness and courtesy have no place in an authoritarian system, as his public words unconsciously revealed. Now, however, things have settled down in the diocese, with no hard feelings on either side. These things are mentioned here not in order to reopen a closed chapter, but simply to illustrate a thesis.

To effect the reforms which the sixteenth-century Reformers failed to effect because they split off and separated themselves from the Church will be agonisingly difficult, and the danger is that if they take too long to implement there will be mass secessions on a large scale, and possibly the creation of new "national" churches independent of Rome. Nothing, in fact, has prepared the psychological climate for such a development more than has the scrapping of the Church's Latin liturgy, which, whatever its drawbacks, was one of the strongest forces making for unity among Catholics.

It is therefore in the best interests of the Holy See that the needed reforms are implemented as quickly as possible.

Unfortunately, the structure of the Church is ill-adapted for the recognition of inconvenient truths and for the implementation of radical reforms. The questions most urgently needing to be dealt with are those of episcopal-clerical relations, secrecy over the making of decisions and their arbitrary imposition, defects of recruitment for the ministry and in its training, habits of blind obedience, lay avoidance of responsibility, and fear of "scandal". Fear of scandal really means fear of losing face through admission of errors, an attitude which seems ingrained in the modern papacy and the papal church. It was this which led a certain prelate, faced with a mounting flood of protest over "Humanae Vitae", to say: "When the Pope issues a decree, whatever we may believe in our hearts, outwardly we must all accept." He no doubt believed this, and said it in all good faith. But the comment was made at the time that this seemed to be a straightforward invitation to people, in certain circumstances, to live a lie. Similarly, Monsignor Lambruschini, the Vatican's official spokesman, said in the *Osservatore della Domenica* that with regard to the encyclical, a Catholic who could not see the reasons for the Pope's decision had no right to challenge it, but must accept it humbly.

The root of the trouble lies in the long-standing way of thinking of canonical and religious obedience as a "blind" obedience—in practice it amounts to an attitude of "My superior, right or wrong"—and still more in a misdeveloped and badly formulated doctrine of papal and ecclesial infallibility. If the Pope's utterances, even those which have nothing whatever to do with revealed doctrine, are invested with quasi-oracular status, then it will be regarded as a kind of treason to question anything the Pontiff says or to suggest that he has sometimes, like any other mortal, made mistakes. From that position, a legend develops that one pope cannot unsay what another has said, so that every kind of shift and manœuvre is resorted to by theologians and apologists to prove that papal doctrine on any subject has a monolithic unity and coherence. In other words, once the Pope has adopted a virtually "infallible" position in matters over which he cannot be infallible, he has either to persist to the point of logical absurdity—as with "Humanae Vitae"—or else to be dishonest, shift the emphasis, and pretend that what was said infallibly before really meant something quite different from, or even quite opposite to, its clear and obvious meaning. Hence all the theologians who are at the present moment busily engaged in demonstrating that "Humanae Vitae" does not really condemn contraception at all. All this, of course, leads to dishonesty, legalism, and moral loathsomeness.

It leads also to absurdities such as the statement of Monsignor Ferdinando Lambruschini, when presenting "Humanae Vitae" at a press conference in Rome, to the effect that the encyclical was not infallible, although it could have been if the Pope had wanted it to be! Could the "oracular" view of papal authority be carried further?

The fact is that the "oracle" view of the papal function has issued in such a series of blunders and follies, from Galileo or earlier onwards, that a high percentage of the educated laity—the clergy are more guarded in expressing themselves—now give the dogma of papal infallibility only a notional or general assent. In 1968 a missionary bishop in India, Francis Simons, published a book, *Infallibility and the Evidence*,[4] in which he argued that the formulation of the dogma had been a mistake and that it should be rescinded. His argument, he claims, "leaves intact the substance of Christianity and the ultimate bases of certainty on which even infallibility must be grounded." As far as I know this book has not been censured in Rome, which is perhaps a hopeful sign.

In a letter to *The Times* on August 13th 1968 Dr Edwin Morris, the retired Archbishop of Wales, asked:

First, who decides whether a papal pronouncement is infallible or not? One Roman view is that only the Pope himself can decide this, which seems to be the logical implication of the infallibility decree of Vatican I. This, however, raises the further question: How does the Pope inform the world that a particular papal pronouncement is infallible? I cannot recall any instance in which this has been done in set terms. Is it permissible to regard as fallible a papal pronouncement which has not been declared by a Pope in set terms to be infallible?

If, on the other hand, the decision whether a particular papal pronouncement is infallible or not rests elsewhere than with the Pope, who has this power of decision; and how is it exercised? The Roman Church has never issued a list of the papal pronouncements that it claims are infallible, so Anglicans and others do not know to what reunion with Rome would commit them in this respect. Infallibility, if it exists, is useless unless it can be certainly known when it has been exercised.

These points are well made. The fact is that as we have it, from Vatican I and II, the dogma of papal infallibility is a dogma that does not "work", and which remains peripheral to the life of the Catholic Christian except for its undeniable nuisance-value as a cause of misgiving to other Christians, and now of disillusionment to Catholics themselves.

And yet, the Fathers of Vatican I were certainly trying to express *something* about the Church and the Pope which is true; something which springs, as Newman emphasised, from the commission to *teach* which Christ gave to the Church. Within the area of her commission to teach all nations the truths revealed to her by God through Christ a certain indefectibility must attach to the Church, otherwise she could not, in the words of St Vincent of Lérins, proceed confidently in her doctrine of God.

It was unfortunate that the word "infallibility" was ever introduced in this connexion. Only one being is infallible, and that is God himself. And since all ideas of revelation and inspiration have to be excluded when considering the Church's infallibility, this "infallibility" must be something other than the oracular quality with which bad theology and superstition have credited the Pope. Since God alone is infallible, and since the decrees of popes and councils are neither inspired nor revealed, the doctrine which they embody will be framed within the limitations of human thought and language, and at least *thus far* will be capable of revision.

Orthodox Christians also believe in the infallibility of the

Church, but their understanding of it is very different from that of the Latins. The Orthodox see infallibility as belonging to the Church in its *theandric totality*. That is, decrees of General Councils —and it is agreed that the Bishop of Rome has the right, as senior patriarch, to preside at General Councils—are accepted by them "conditionally" as soon as they are promulgated; but they are not recognised as formally expressing the faith of the Church until such time as it becomes clear from the *consensus fidelium* that they do in fact express the mind of the whole Church.

A similar view is now gaining ground in the Latin church as a result of the new thinking about collegiality. Thus Dr B. C. Butler, the former Abbot of Downside, now an auxiliary bishop in the diocese of Westminster, has said:

> The kind of knowledge of God and Christ which is possible for us in this life is a knowledge by faith. The content of our faith is Christ himself, the living Word of God. And Christ is he who indwells the whole Church. His presence was not entrusted to a privileged section of the Church—e.g., the Pope or the episcopal-apostolic college. It was given to the whole Church, and constitutes that whole Church as his body. We owe our faith not to the magisterium but to the Church. Our faith is not exclusively the faith of the Pope, or of the bishops. It is the faith of us all, and is shared in by the bishops, including the Bishop of Rome, on the same terms as we share it.
>
> . . . What the episcopate thus proclaims is the tradition as it lives, not just in the minds of the bishops, but in the whole life of the Church. The episcopate has no private source of information about Christ. Like the rest of us, the bishops derive their knowledge of him from the Church as a whole. . . . Neither the Pope as such, nor the episcopal college as such, is the recipient of special revelation from on high.[5]

If the present unsatisfactory formulations of infallibility are not simply to be quietly shelved, and an attempt is to be made to reinterpret them in a more adequate way, the final definition arrived at, covering the whole question of the position of the Pope in the Church, and his prerogatives, must surely be made in terms that combine what is true in both the Conciliarist and Papalist positions.

The Conciliarists were concerned that the Pope's pre-eminence should be defined as being within, but not above, the Church. Among the most eminent Conciliarists, though he later modified his views, was the illustrious cardinal Nicholas of Cusa (1401–1464), who in his *De concordantia catholica* stated: "Nec fuit Petrus ex illo primatu ecclesiae maior, quoniam ipse ab ecclesia et propter eam nominatur. . . . Quare illa Petri maioritas non fuit maioritas supra sed intra ecclesiam."[6] The cardinal argued that the Church is a fraternity of believers, a living unity of souls in fellowship with Christ. An order of connexion is necessary, and this is provided by the hierarchy. In each diocese the bishop represents and assures the unity of the Church, the unity of the whole is assured and represented by the Pope. Because the primacy belongs to the see of Rome, it is the right of the Pope to summon a General Council, and it would not be a General Council if it did not include the Pope or his legates. But if the Pope disassociates himself from a General Council properly assembled, the Council may continue its work for the good of the Church, though it should always treat the Pope with the utmost deference, and never decide without him upon dogmatic questions. If, however, the Pope proves unfaithful, the Council must anathematise him, and withdraw from his obedience; in that case, the Pope is deposed. Since it represents the universal Church, a General Council has its authority immediately from Christ and is above both the Pope himself personally and the Apostolic See.[7]

In the last resort it does seem that this must be so. For how otherwise, for example, can schisms due to rival claimants to the papacy be resolved? In 1415 the Council of Constance (see p. 58 *supra*) eliminated three rival claimants and elected Martin V in their place, and then passed the decree *Sacrosancta* affirming the superiority of General Councils over the Pope. The Council of Constance has an irrefutable title to be recognised as ecumenical, in the Latin understanding of the term, and its findings and actions ought to be more widely known.

And how can faulty papal pronouncements on matters of

doctrine be corrected except by a General Council? A pope is not likely to correct himself, and there can be no certainty that his successor will correct him. The case of Pope John XXII comes to mind. On All Saints' Day 1331 this pope preached a sermon on the subject of the Beatific Vision which contained views which were at once recognised as unorthodox. An English Dominican, Thomas Waleys, preached against these views in the Pope's own city of Avignon, and was imprisoned for his pains. The Pope was also opposed, chiefly for other views of his which were deemed unorthodox, by the English Franciscan William of Ockham. Many Franciscans, because of his alleged heresies, no longer recognised John as a lawful pope, and referred to him simply as "James of Cahors". But pope or no pope, John XXII refused to modify his views on the Beatific Vision, and it was left to his successor Benedict XII to restate the orthodox doctrine. But supposing he had not been willing to do so, the only way of settling the matter would have been through a General Council.

Apart from emergencies, such as that with which the Council of Constance was faced, the normal procedure in major matters of Church government should be for the Pope and the bishops to work together, in personal collaboration. This seems to be the meaning of Vatican II's statement on episcopal collegiality; but it is timidly expressed, and hedged about with reservations, in the form of "modi" inserted on the instruction of the Pope himself, which water down the attempt of the bishops to assert their proper rights. The Pope has said subsequently that in the present disturbed state of the Church he has no intention of governing collegially, since the risks involved are too great. The Pope also made it clear at his consistory of May 1st 1969 that the functions both of the college of cardinals and of the episcopal synod are "essentially consultative" and subordinate. The Pope referred, in fact, to his "prerogative of personal, universal, and direct government". At the Synod of Bishops held in Rome in October 1969 the Pope, under pressure, retreated somewhat from his rigid anti-collegial attitude; but essentially the position remains unchanged.

Latin theologians are handicapped in their attempts to define that quality in the Church which they call "infallibility" by the limitations of their thought-forms and their language, their inadequate knowledge and understanding of Church history, which for most of them is simply *Latin* church history, and above all because they are not able to draw on the theological traditions and insights of the Eastern churches. The question of reunion with the East is now much discussed in the West; but it is, and always will be, totally impossible for the Easterns to accept the absolutist Latin papacy with its claim to universal jurisdiction, and the doctrine of papal infallibility as defined in 1870. Is there any way out of the impasse? Yes, there is. There is one way, and it would seem one only.

It rests on the fact, now widely accepted among both Catholics and Orthodox, and not seriously disputed except by a few on either side, that the historic universal Church of primitive Christendom is represented today by the Roman Catholic Church and the Orthodox Church together, although *de facto* they have not been in communion with one another for a very long time. Their juridical separation, under which a sacramental unity has persisted, has at no time involved any excommunication of one church by the other. Humbert of Silva Candida's excommunication of the patriarch Michael Cerularius in 1054, and the patriarch's excommunication of Humbert and the other papal legates, have now been solemnly revoked by Pope Paul VI and the Ecumenical Patriarch Athenagoras, who have met in Rome and in Constantinople. There is only one church of Christ, and it comprises the Eastern and Western churches together.

If this is so,[8] then, since a General or Ecumenical Council is an assembly of bishops from *all* the churches, it follows that there has been no truly ecumenical council since the Second Council of Nicaea in the year 787. (This is, in fact, the last council to be generally admitted as ecumenical by both East *and* West.)

If there have been no ecumenical councils since 787, then all councils held since then under papal authority have been General Synods of the Latin church, and nothing more.

The Latin church is part of the Church but not the whole. Since a part of the Church cannot legislate for the whole Church, the decrees of councils at which the Eastern church is not properly represented are unilateral, because they are made by one part of the Church only, and therefore have authority for that part alone.

It is no accident that since the "Schism" the East has never defined or promulgated any dogmas, since to do so without the West would be a unilateral action, and hence invalid with respect to the whole Church.

This simple and surely unassailable proposition is the key to the question of reunion between East and West.

Let the West officially acknowledge this to be the position, and then, having done so, the Pope can convene the first ecumenical council for over eleven centuries.

The task of this Ecumenical Council of Reunion would be to work out for the Church a new constitution, which would recognise in the Bishop of Rome such a primacy as was recognised to be his in the primitive, undivided church; it would regulate the exercise of the Pope's primacy by canon, and distinguish it clearly from the powers of jurisdiction which are the Pope's in his own bishopric and patriarchate. The papal primacy, although recognised in the East as well as in the West, has never been defined by a truly ecumenical council. In arriving at such a definition the Council of Reunion would have to take into account the decrees of Vatican I and II, but it would not be bound by them since they were passed unilaterally by the Latin church and stand in need of correction. The Council would assure their full rights and privileges to the patriarchs, which would include precedence over the cardinals of the Roman church. The Synod of Bishops would become a deliberative instead of merely consultative body, and in working out a satisfactory system of collegial church government a special rôle might well be allotted to the Pentarchy. The decree *Frequens* of the Council of Constance would be promulgated once more, and General Councils held regularly as it enjoins.

It would be defined that the supreme authority in the Church, both in matters of doctrine and of government, is the General Council (as was declared by the Council of Constance); but there would be nothing anti-papal in this definition since it is admitted by all that the Pope is an integral part of the Council, and that he has a right to convoke the Council and preside at it, and that its decrees are not normally valid unless signed by himself as well as by the other bishops present. The primacy of the Pope would not be questioned, but only, and for the first time, properly defined by a council of the whole Church.

The Church's pattern for its higher government would then conform to the pattern of government which is traditional in the government of the Church's religious orders. Each religious order has a supreme head, known as the Master General (Dominicans), Prior General (Carmelites), or Minister General (Franciscans), or by some equivalent title. The General of a religious order is elected by an assembly, the General Chapter, which is representative of the members of the Order all over the world. Once elected, the General enjoys a true primacy both of honour and of jurisdiction within the Order, but his powers are well defined and are not absolute. The control of the Order and its affairs are in his hands, but he is bound to hold regular meetings of his Council (also an elected body), without whose consent there are many matters in which he cannot proceed. He is responsible to the General Chapter, the Order's supreme legislative body, and must give an account of his stewardship to the Chapter whenever it assembles, which will not be less than once in six years, and may well be more frequently. The Chapter can dismiss the Superior General if he has been found defective in carrying out his duties, and will in any case elect his successor after a General has resigned or died.

This method of government works well as long as the system of voting for the General of an Order is functioning properly. In orders where, for example, very poor provinces are dependent on subsidies and benefactions from rich ones, rich provinces can virtually command the votes of poor ones for their own candidates. Gerrymandering of this kind is not unknown. If an Order has a run of Generals of the same nationality it can reasonably be suspected that some such factor as this is at work. But allowing for the imperfections which may become manifest in all systems of government, this one works well, since it gives real authority and responsibility to the man at the top, but with safeguards to ensure that his authority is not absolute; and it places the final control of the Order's affairs and destinies in the hands of a representative body meeting at regular intervals.

It is quite unthinkable that supreme power over the members of a religious order should be invested *absolutely* in one man; *pari passu* and *a fortiori*, it seems impossible that this should have been Christ's intention for the government of his Church. To say so much is not at all to deny the primacy of Peter among the Apostles or the primacy of the Pope among the bishops; it is merely to question that particular view of the primacy which has been dominant in the Latin church, except for a few brief periods, at least from the time of Leo the Great. This view has led to such mischievous notions as the idea, still widely held, that the Pope is the "ordinary" of all the faithful, so that the authority of bishops and parish priests comes directly from the Pope, who can restrict or abolish it as he pleases.

With papal authority functioning *within* that of conciliar church government, the Pope would then be seen as truly the successor of St Peter in pastoral care, and as a centre of reference and a source of unity for the whole Church. The Church, at peace in her new-found unity, would then appear as the city set on a hill whose light shines before men, guiding them into the way of truth. Free from dissensions and anxieties within herself the Church would be able to fulfil with a new assurance and dedication her rôle of builder of the kingdom of Christ, "A kingdom of truth and life: a kingdom of sanctity and grace: a kingdom of justice, love, and peace."[9]

Pope Hadrian the Seventh would have agreed. In his bull "Regnum Meum" this pope said:[10]

We use worldly things till they are wanted by the world: then we will relinquish them without even so much as a backward thought. For we are all clearly marked to get that which we give. Nothing is irrevocable on this orb of earth. Nothing is final: for, after this world is the world to come. Therefore let us move, let us move gladly, move with the times, really move.

Finis

APPENDIX A

THE WIDER ECUMENISM

THIS book has examined certain aspects of the sickness which now afflicts the Roman Catholic church, especially in the matter of Church authority. But the sickness goes deeper than this; it is more than a question of the malfunctioning of hierarchic structures. Faults in Church organisation should not be too difficult to repair; what makes the present sickness of the Catholic Church a sickness almost unto death is the fact that ultimately it is a sickness of *religion*.

What do we mean by religion? The word has more than one meaning; none of those offered by, for instance, the *Concise Oxford Dictionary* is satisfactory, though each of them expresses something of what the word means in ordinary thought and speech. Personally, I like the definition offered by Rodney Collin:[1] "Religion means the art of becomingly consciously rejoined to God." This links up with St Thomas Aquinas's explanation, which is apparently etymologically faulty, that the word religion comes from the Latin *religare*, meaning to bind together again or reunite.

According, again, to the *Concise Oxford Dictionary*, art means, basically, skill; and skill means expertise, practical ability of some kind. This presupposes a work to be done or something to be made; and the Scholastics, as Eric Gill and Jacques Maritain used to remind us, have defined art as the *recta ratio factibilium*; that is, the right making of things that need making.

A slightly archaic phrase speaks of a man "making his soul"; a work that is usually envisaged as taking place towards the end of a man's or a woman's life, when death is sensed, if not to be imminent, at least to be approaching. But the making of our soul ought to be a lifelong task.

It is, in fact, the principal task of a human life; which means that religion should be the most important element in man's life from birth to death.

The major religious traditions of mankind all teach that man is in some way out of tune with the infinite; that in the rhythm and harmony of the cosmos man somehow introduces a discordant note; so that his innate desire for happiness—for goodness, beauty, and truth—can be fulfilled only by the re-creation in himself of this shattered harmony. As Article ix of the Articles of Religion puts it: Original Sin "is the fault and corruption of the Nature of every man that naturally is engendered of the offspring of *Adam*: whereby every man is very far gone from original righteousness, and is of his own nature inclined to evil . . ."

Man's "original righteousness" is seen in biblical terms as his being created in the image and likeness of God, and in his sharing in and reflecting the goodness of God. If we like to think of God as Eternal Consciousness, then we must suppose that all created consciousnesses ought to be in perfect union and harmony with the supreme consciousness which is their source. If they are not, it can only be because Eternal Being allows an element of *becoming* to enter into its "external" creation; and that this element of becoming, or of evolution, requires that for certain higher creatures "personal" union with the divine is something that has to be *attained*, since man, at any rate, when he receives existence does so at an epistemic distance from his Creator.

If this is so, it means that those old theologies which associate man's "fallen" state in some way with his freedom are on the right track. Whether freedom is something that man has lost or something to which he has not yet attained makes little difference. What matters is that man should recognise, in whatever words he may express it, his "fallen" state—that is, his blindness, his ignorance, his unfreedom, his capacity for and bias towards wrong thought and action—and that he should set to work to recover or to attain that harmony and integrity which is proper to him as a child of God.

The art or skill which we must exercise if we are to succeed in this task is what we call religion. To think of religion as a purely speculative matter, which may be left to a select few whose temperament especially inclines them to it, or as a mere notional acceptance of certain doctrines and moral precepts, is to degrade the idea of religion.

On God's side, if we may so speak, what *we* call religion is *revelation*; just as the moment to moment conservation of our being which we experience is on God's side *creation*. There is no such thing as "natural religion"; what we mean by this term is a matter of philosophy. Religion in any authentic sense connotes revelation. All authentic religious traditions claim to be the guardians and teachers of certain primal truths about man and his destiny which man in his "fallen" state of ignorance and self-absorption is either morally or absolutely incapable of apprehending. In the major monotheistic traditions, those of Judaism, Christianity, and Islam, and at least in certain schools of Hindu thought, these primal truths are believed to come by way of divine revelation. In Buddhism they seem to be thought of rather as some kind of residual cosmic wisdom; but they are still revealed truths in the sense that the earthly "natural" man cannot of his own power attain to them, but must, ordinarily, receive them from one who is himself "enlightened". In Christian terms, man's restoration to a state of primal integrity and "innocence" is a matter of *grace*.

Christianity has seemed for many centuries past, perhaps almost from its inception, to claim to be the *sole* revelation of God to man, Judaism being allowed, obviously, a genuine revelationary rôle in the centuries before Christ, but being now considered to have no further relevance, and the faith of Islam being regarded as at best a heresy or deviation from Christianity. No element of the divine was allowed to the Asian religions, nor to the beliefs of Greece and Rome, ancient Egypt, the Incas and Aztecs, and other "pagans".

This attitude was never entirely universal in Christendom. In the Middle Ages the lines beginning

> *Sicelides Musae, paullo majora canamus:*
> (Sicilian Muse, begin a loftier strain!)

in Virgil, *Bucolic IV*, were widely held to be an authentic prophecy of Christ's coming, and the medievals' virtual canonisation of Virgil is well known. But the characteristic attitude of Christians during these and later centuries was that of the Crusaders, with their hatred and contempt for Mohammed, and of St Francis Xavier, for whom all the sacred images in Indian temples were "idols" to be hacked to pieces. This was not, however, the attitude of the early Christian apologist St Justin Martyr (*c.* A.D. 100–165), who says in the first book of his *Apology* for the Christian faith:

> But lest any, to turn men from our teaching, should attack us with the unreasonable argument that we say that Christ was born one hundred and fifty years ago in the time of Cyrenius, and that he taught what we affirm he taught thereafter in the time of Pontius Pilate, if, I say, they should find fault with us for treating as irresponsible all men born before him, let us solve this difficulty by anticipation. We are taught that Christ is the first-born of God, and we have shown above that he is the reason (Word) of whom the whole human race partake, and those who live according to reason are Christians, even though they are accounted atheists. Such were Socrates and Heraclitus among the Greeks, and those like them. . . .

And in the second book of his *Apology* Justin says:

> Whatever has been uttered aright by any men in any place belongs to us Christians; for, next to God, we worship and love the reason (Word) which is from the unbegotten and ineffable God; since on our account he has been made man, so that, being made partaker of our sufferings, he may also bring us healing. For all the ancient authors were able to see the truth darkly, through the implanted seed of reason (the Word) dwelling in them.

What Justin is here saying had already been affirmed by the writer of the Fourth Gospel, in his prologue, when he identified Jesus Christ, the Word of God, who had been made flesh and dwelt among us, with the light "which lighteneth every man coming into the world" (John i, 9).

In virtue of the Second Vatican Council's Declaration ("Nostra Aetate") on the Relationship of the Church to Non-Christian Religions the Church has now adopted a standpoint which is very close to the early Christian thought of Justin Martyr. The Declaration, which is worth citing at some length, says that

> From ancient times down to the present there has existed among diverse peoples a certain perception of that hidden power which hovers over the course of things and over the events of human life; at times, indeed, recognition can be found of a Supreme Divinity and of a Supreme Father too. Such a perception and such a recognition instill the lives of these peoples with a profound religious sense. Religions bound up with cultural advancement have struggled to reply to these same questions with more refined concepts and in more highly developed language.
>
> Thus in Hinduism men contemplate the divine mystery and express it through an unspent fruitfulness of myths and through searching philosophical inquiry. They seek release from the anguish of our condition through ascetical practices or deep meditation, or a loving, trusting flight towards God.
>
> Buddhism in its multiple forms acknowledges the radical insufficiency of this shifting world. It teaches a path by which men, in a devout and confident spirit, can either reach a state of absolute freedom or attain supreme enlightenment by their own efforts or by higher assistance.
>
> Likewise, other religions to be found everywhere strive variously to answer the restless searchings of the human heart by proposing "ways", which consist of teachings, rules of life, and sacred ceremonies.
>
> The Catholic Church rejects nothing which is true and holy in these religions. . . .

Upon the Moslems too the Church looks with esteem. They adore one God, living and enduring, merciful and all-powerful, Maker of heaven and earth, who speaks to men. They strive to submit wholeheartedly to his inscrutable decrees as did Abraham, with whom the faith of Islam associates itself. . . . Although in the course of the centuries many quarrels and hostilities have arisen between Christians and Moslems, this most sacred Synod urges all to forget the past and to strive sincerely for mutual understanding. On behalf of all mankind, let them make common cause for safeguarding and fostering social justice, moral values, peace, and freedom.

As this sacred Synod searches into the mystery of the Church, it recalls the spiritual bond which links the people of the New Covenant with the stock of Abraham. For the Church of Christ acknowledges that, according to the mystery of God's saving design, the beginnings of her faith and her election are already found among the patriarchs, Moses, and the prophets. She professes that all who believe in Christ, Abraham's sons according to faith, are included in the same patriarch's call, and likewise that the salvation of the Church was mystically foreshadowed by the chosen people's exodus from the land of bondage.

The Church repudiates all persecutions against any man. Moreover, mindful of her common patrimony with the Jews, and motivated by the gospel's spirit of love, and by no political considerations, she deplores the hatred, persecutions, and displays of antisemitism directed against the Jews at any time and from any source.

In its opening paragraph the Declaration states that the Church is giving deeper study to her relationship with non-Christian religions, and that she wishes in this context to give consideration to what men of different faiths have in common and to what promotes fellowship among them. This wider ecumenism is of the greatest importance for the future of man, since it seems to be the religious traditions of mankind alone that can prevent the disaster which must follow if the notion of a traditional and human society is universally rejected in favour of a society based on technology, science, and industry. A traditional society is one in which "every aspect and action of human life has a ritual character opening possibilities of spiritual development" to those who follow the tradition.[2] Modern technology, science, and industry are universally destructive of the "ritual" character of human life, and offer man no possibilities of spiritual development, but rather the opposite.[3] Hence the lack of interest in and contempt for religion which characterises modern man.

There is little chance of preventing the dehumanisation of man and the disasters which must follow from ruthless scientific and industrial exploitation of the natural resources of our planet as long as the religious traditions of mankind are divided from each other by mutual hostility and misunderstanding, and as long as Christianity itself is divided and cannot speak with an assured voice.

Among Catholics the technological outlook has won such general acceptance that it has led to the destruction of the Latin church's greatest treasure, its traditional liturgy, with a consequent elimination of symbolism and ritual, now thought to be "useless", from that Church's public worship.

The Eastern churches, whose sense of eternity is in sharp distinction with the Western Christian's concern with time and "up-to-dateness", are conscious of the vital importance of the traditional forms of public worship, in language, ritual, and music, which now constitute a strong bulwark against the total destruction of the Christian tradition. Hence the urgency of reunion between East and West. Since the Orthodox churches have four patriarchs and the Latin church only one, if reunion were effected, and the Pentarchy restored, under the Pope's presidency, as the ultimate authority in Church government when a General Council is not sitting, there would be some hope of the decay of traditional Western Christianity being halted and a renewal of Catholicism being implemented.

THE NEW ENGLISH LITURGY

THE capricious way in which authority is exercised by the papacy in its present state of imbalance is nowhere more clearly seen than in its iron rigidity in the matter of birth control and its permissiveness in the matter of liturgy. In November 1969 the Pope is still trying to enforce the teaching of "Humanae Vitae", as though that "ill-prepared document with at least two authors"[1] could be identified with the authentic voice of the Church. Forty priests suspended over a year ago by the Cardinal Archbishop of Boston, because of their declared dissent from the encyclical, remain suspended; and in the English diocese of Nottingham four priests still remain suspended.

There are now so many different ways in which Mass may be said, and seemingly there are more to come, and the translations authorised for use in England are so bad, that all sense of the numinous in divine worship is now lost and the services in Roman Catholic churches are often of a tedium and banality that one would not have thought possible.

Fortunately, the Mass of the Roman rite as published under the authority of the Pope St Pius V has still not actually been abrogated.[2] But the most surprising thing about the wholesale and ill-advised changes now being implemented is the way they have been accepted by the clergy of the Latin rite almost without protest. The laity have been far more vocal in showing their dissatisfaction; another reason for regarding them as at present the healthiest part of the Church.

The selection of texts which follows is offered as food for reflection, especially to Anglicans, whom one may hope will exercise great caution before adopting into their own liturgy any of the recently authorised Roman changes.

Article 36 (1) Particular law remaining in force, the use of the Latin language is to be preserved in the Latin rites.

(2) But since the use of the mother tongue, whether in the Mass, the administration of the sacraments, or other parts of the liturgy, may frequently be of great advantage to the people, the limits of its employments may be extended.

Vatican II, Constitution on the Sacred Liturgy, 4 December 1963.

Modern humanity is not even able to imagine how profoundly the magic of word and speech was experienced in ancient civilizations and the enormous influence it had on the entire life, especially in its religious aspects.

Lama Anagarika Govinda, *Foundations of Tibetan Mysticism*: Rider and Co., 1967, p. 19.

Now no one will deny that there is, in English . . . a liturgical language which should be employed in corporate worship. The Prayer Book has created this. But it is not the same thing as Tudor English. Later epochs have contributed to it; and there is no reason why the twentieth century should not have a worthy contribution to make to it.

Walter Howard Frere, sometime Bishop of Truro: cited in *The Language of the Book of Common Prayer* by Stella Brook: André Deutsch, 1965, p. 208.

The ancient and venerable text of the Roman Canon has been mutilated beyond recognition. The ruling idea seems to have been to see how much could be cut out on any pretext or none. This certainly is not what Rome had in mind when it demanded a version "without mutilations or simplifications of any kind".

The Tablet, leading article, 9.12.1967

Surely the Mass should be treated with as much respect as the major European poems, and demands the same professional loyalty.

Mr Bernard Wall, letter in *The Tablet*, 9.12.1967

Will the changes, no matter how well intended, but entailing so vast a loss, aid us, conditioned as we are to this or that degree by the desacramentalised world in which we chance to live, to be more drawn towards those "things unseen"? That is the question. . . . This document confirms the worst apprehensions. Every vestige of sacred beauty has gone by the board, and its numerous omissions are more ominous still.

Dr David Jones, CH: letter in *The Tablet*, 2.12.1967

In the name of reform a beautiful and dignified rite which did indeed raise the heart and mind to God is being wantonly destroyed.

Miss Alexandra Zaina, letter in *The Times*, Nov. 1967

I shall never understand why the Roman Catholic Church will not adopt an English liturgy based on Cranmer's translations.

Mr Francis G. Walker (Eliot College, The University, Canterbury), letter in *The Times*, 11,11,1967

In the absence of loud complaint or protest the clergy very naturally believe that the laity as a whole are as eager as they are to abandon the old service; they have no idea of the hold which the 1662 liturgy has upon the hearts of ordinary church people. So did the authorities of the Roman Catholic Church misjudge the feelings of many of the laity over the change from the Latin Mass to Mass in the vernacular, a change which has been much less popular than might have been expected.

Mrs Georgina Battiscombe, "The Destruction of Common Prayer", in *Theology*, February 1968.

The non-rational factors in the Mass were almost the last effective means available for counteracting the one-sided personalistic philosophy of Western man and vitalising in his soul that gift of faith which is not of the conscious mind but is the fruit of a direct experience of the divine Numen. It is the greatest tragedy of our century that Catholicism, the last of the great mystery religions, has made concessions to the profane mind that almost banish from the liturgy that compensatory transpersonal power which alone can take human personality captive and transform it into a supra-personal alliance with God.

Mr John Silk, article "De Profundis" in *The Aylesford Review*, Summer 1968.

We have witnessed with immense sorrow the decay of ritual in the Church of Rome—the neglect of church music and the slovenly attitude of priests towards ceremonial—but we had hoped the English Church would continue to conduct its public worship in a manner befitting man's corporate worship of his maker and his Saviour, present in the Blessed Sacrament.

But, it seems, "modern" Anglican priests will not rest content until they have converted their churches into Protestant preaching houses and have relegated all beautiful ceremonial and music to the House of Lords and the concert hall! Their new creed tells them that candles and lamps must be discarded, nave altars must be erected,

Mass must be celebrated facing the congregation, and that all mystery and dignity must be ousted by harshness and vulgarity.

However, the new iconoclasts have not succeeded yet in smashing down the Catholic faith completely. Several societies such as ours now exist to counter these pernicious and destructive movements within the Church of England, and to promote the preservation and restoration of the full Catholic Prayer Book ritual, in all its magnificent solemnity, throughout our Communion. We are, indeed, concerned to "communicate"; but we believe, with Seneca, that man believes his eyes rather than he believes his ears. Catholic Christendom must speak to man through his eyes as well as his ears if its worship is not to degenerate into the sour and barren coldness that is Puritanism.

Letter from the Chairman and Treasurer of The Cambridge Ecclesiological Society in *The Spectator*, 21.6.1969.

THE COUNCIL OF CONSTANCE
(NOVEMBER 5 1414—April 22 1418)

ROMAN CATHOLIC historians usually betray a certain embarrassment when treating of the Council of Constance. They are not prepared to deny its ecumenicity (by Latin standards), but make every kind of shift to exclude the decrees *Sacrosancta* and *Frequens* from the Council's authoritative pronouncements. Thus the late Mgr Philip Hughes in his *The Church in Crisis: a History of the General Councils: 325–1870* (New York, Doubleday, 1960) says that "After Constance things were never the same again . . . The ecclesiastical system, the system based on the hitherto unquestioned general assumption of the pope's right to rule the whole Church as its earthly master, this had there received a blow in the face . . ." This seems less than candid, for the totalitarian view of the papacy had not gone previously unquestioned in the West and had always been repudiated in the East.

The Council of Constance was convened by John XXIII, the Pisan pope, but at the instigation of King Sigismund, the Emperor-elect. A minority of Catholic scholars, who can make out a strong case for their belief, holds that the Council was ecumenical (in Western terms) from the beginning. Those who dissent from this view acknowledge that it was ecumenical at least from July 1415 when it was reconvoked by Gregory XII (the Roman pope) prior to his abdication.

The Council has been described as 'the greatest representative assembly of medieval Christendom.' In the course of its three and a half years' duration it was attended by 3 patriarchs, 29 cardinals, 33 archbishops, over 300 bishops and over 100 abbots, 12 ruling princes, and several hundred doctors of divinity and canon law.

Ultramontanes naturally attempt to show that Martin V, the pope finally elected by the Council, did not approve its decrees *Sacrosancta* and *Frequens*; however, Brian Tierney says in his article on the Council of Constance in *The Catholic Encyclopaedia* (New York, 1966): "It seems most probable that Martin V did express his approval of *Sacrosancta*".

APPENDIX D

CLERICAL CELIBACY

THE author's views on clerical celibacy have not been affected by the *Instruction* of the Sacred Congregation for the Clergy sent to bishops' conferences of the Latin Rite on 4 November 1969 and made public on 9 February 1970.

The *Instruction* directs that all priests are to make a public renewal of their vows of celibacy and obedience once a year, on Maundy Thursday, and insists also on an intensified training for priests *after their ordination*, with special reference to obedience to the Pope and the bishops. "By divine institution", the document says, "the task of teaching the truths of the faith belongs to the Pope and the bishops in communion with him, and not to laymen or priests. The decisions proposed by the Magisterium [the Church's teaching authority] must be accepted loyally, without exceptions or subterfuge, otherwise everything would be pointless and valueless." (*Times* report, 10.2.1970.)

The clear implications of this are that the faithful, both lay and clerical, have no share whatever in the formulation of doctrine, or even in the enacting of the Church's code of discipline so that everything emanating from the pontifical magisterium must be accepted without question. This is simply a new iteration of the old, and heterodox, notion of the Pope as oracle.

The document is put out on the authority of the intransigent American Cardinal Wright, formerly bishop of Pittsburgh, so that its tone and trend need surprise no one. It cannot but cause further bitterness and dismay among the lower clergy and laity of the Latin Church, already sharply divided as a result of *Humanae Vitae*.

ABBREVIATIONS

CL = *Actorum et Decretorum S. Conciliorum Recentiorum Collectio Lacensis*, Freiburg-im-Breisgau 1870ff.

Corp. jur. civ. = *Corpus juris civilis*, ed. Kruger-Mommsen: Berlin, 1889ff.

DTC = *Dictionnaire de théologie catholique*: Paris, Letouzey, 1920ff.

Mansi = *Sacrorum Conciliorum Nova et Amplissima Collectio*, ed. G. B. Mansi: 31 vols., Florence, 1759–98.

Migne PL = *Patrologia Latina*, ed. J. P. Migne: 221 vols., Paris, 1844–1864.

Migne PG = *Patrologia Graeca*, ed. J. P. Migne, 162 vols., Paris, 1857–1866.

Quotations from the decrees of the Second Vatican Council are mostly given in the translations provided in *The Documents of Vatican II* edited by Walter M. Abbott, S.J.: London, Geoffrey Chapman, 1966.

In the original edition of *The Microscope of the New Testament* by the present author's Tractarian kinsman Dr William Sewell the scriptural quotations are given in Greek characters. As a concession to the modern reader they are here transliterated into Roman characters.

INTRODUCTION

1. Collegiality: Vatican II teaches that "Just as, by the Lord's will, St Peter and the other Apostles constituted one apostolic college,

so in a similar way the Roman Pontiff as the successor of St Peter, and the bishops as the successors of the apostles are joined together. ... Together with its head the Roman Pontiff, and never without this head, the episcopal order is the subject of supreme and full power over the universal Church." *Dogmatic Constitution on the Church ("Lumen Gentium"), section 22.*

2. *The Universe:* a popular Roman Catholic weekly of large circulation.

3. Priest-dissenters are bound, quite properly, not to preach against the encyclical, and in counselling people they are bound to state plainly the papal teaching. They are not required to defend it if they cannot in conscience do so.

4. Cf. two articles under the heading "The Primacy of Peter" by Father Cornelius Ernest, O.P., in *New Blackfriars* for April and May 1969. Briefly, Father Ernst is concerned to explore in these articles the possibility of discovering the elements of what he calls a theology of an *ontological* primacy of Peter which could balance or even replace the jurisdictional and "political" theology of the papal primacy which found its most balanced expression in the decrees of the First Vatican Council.

These two articles are more "revolutionary" than the article for which an editor of *New Blackfriars* was dismissed two years previously; but they have met with no censure: a sign that some progress has been made since August 1968 in the matter of freedom within the Latin Church for genuine theological research and debate.

1 SAINT PETER IN THE NEW TESTAMENT

1. "Percontatus est ex eo utrumnam cum episcopis catholicis, hoc est cum romana ecclesia, conveniret." Ambrose, *De excessu fratris Satyri*, I, 47.

2. Strype, *Ecclesiastical Memorials*, 1822, vol. iii, pt 2, pp. 491–3.

3. Batiffol, *Le Siège Apostolique:* 359–451: Paris, Gabalda, 1924: p. 593.

4. Bramhall, *Works*, pp. 399–400.

5. London, SPCK, 1944: p. 528.

6. Cf. *The New Testament Witness to St Peter* by Fr Vincent McNabb, O.P., S.T.M. (London, Sheed and Ward, 1928).

7. In *Theology* for August and October 1926.

8. Cullmann, *Peter: Disciple: Apostle: Martyr*: London SCM, 1962.

9. Brooke Foss Westcott (1825–1901), Bishop of Durham; sometime Regius Professor of Divinity at Cambridge.

10. *The Microscope of the New Testament* by William Sewell, D.D., edited by W. J. Crichton, M.A.: London, Oxford, Cambridge, Rivingtons, 1878.

11. "Our present position in relation to the Church of Rome . . . is not such as to warrant any expression, or any silence, which may tend to throw weak minds off their guard, and make them insensible to the real enormities of the Romish system."—William Sewell, *A Letter to the Reverend E. B. Pusey* (1841).

12. *Church Times*, 15 December 1922, p. 651.

13. J. B. Lightfoot (1828–1889), Bishop of Durham and sometime Lady Margaret Professor of Divinity at Cambridge.

2 THE CHAIR OF PETER

1. Maxwell Staniforth, *Early Christian Writings—the Apostolic Fathers*: London, Penguin Books, 1968.

2. Batiffol, *Primitive Catholicism*, p. 411.

3. Batiffol, *Le Siège Apostolique*: 359–451: Paris, Gabalda, 1924.

4. Irenaeus *Contra Haereses*, lib. 3, cap. 3: Migne *PL*. 7, 848–9.

5. Cf. F. Dvornik, *Byzance et la Primauté Romaine*: Paris, Editions du Cerf, 1961.

6. Migne, *PL*, 54: 10003.

7. Migne, *PL*, 54: 998–9.

8. Letter to the Emperor Anastasius I: Migne, *PL*, 59: 42–3.

9. A reference to The Tome of Leo.

10. Migne, *PL*, 63: 460.

11. Quoted in Dvornik, *Byzance et la primauté romaine*, from Kroll, *Corpus iuris civilis*, vol. 3, pp. 35ff.

12. *Codex Justiniani* I, 1, 7; in *Corpus jur. civ.*, p. 8.

13. Quoted by Dvornik, *Byzance et la primauté romaine*, p. 64.

14. "My kingdom is not of this world" (John xviii, 36).

15. The text is in Mansi, vol. 12: 1056ff.

16. This title, however, was not meant as a claim to jurisdiction outside the patriarchate, and implied no rejection of the primacy of the Holy See. Pope St Gregory the Great, when the Patriarch of Alexandria addressed him as "universal pope", replied: "If your Holiness styles me universal pope, you deny your own status as bishop, in supposing that I am universal. May God not will it. Far be it from us to use words which inflate pride and offend charity."

17. Mansi, vol. ii, 670–671; Hefele-Leclerc, *Histoire des Conciles*, t. i, p. 552.

18. Spacil, *Conceptus et doctrina de Ecclesia juxta theologiam Orientis separati*, cited in article "Patriarcats" by R. Vancourt: *DTC*, t. xi, 2me partie, 1932.

19. Cited in Dvornik, *Byzance et la primauté romaine*.

20. Mansi, t. 16: 7.

21. This is not to deny the possibility of circumstances in which the Pope could properly act alone; but they would be likely to be rare, and confined, as a rule, to states of emergency.

22. Quoted in George Every, *Misunderstandings between East and West*: London, Lutterworth Press, 1965.

23. Petrus Damianus, *Opusculum Trigesimum Octavum contra errorem Graecorum de processione Spiritus Sancti*: Migne, *PL*: 145, 653ff.

24. I have not yet had an opportunity of reading Robert Markus's and Eric John's book *Papacy and Hierarchy* (London, Sheed and Ward, 1969) which is largely concerned with the influence of the Gregorian Reform or Hildebrandine Revolution on the history of the papacy. Reviewing this book in *Sobornost* for Summer 1969 the Archimandrite Kallistos Timothy Ware indicates that the authors, both of them Roman Catholics, believe that the encyclical "Humanae Vitae" will probably prove to be the death-warrant of the Gregorian and post-Gregorian conception of papal authority. By reverting to an extreme form of authoritarianism, in the Gregorian mode, the Pope has demonstrated that this form of church government and of doctrinal formulation no longer works.

25. Walter Ullmann, *Medieval Papalism*: London, Methuen, 1949: pp. 78–9.

26. Giorgio Falco, *The Holy Roman Republic*, translated by E. V. Kent: London, Allen and Unwin, 1964.

27. I.e., the doctrine of papal "infallibility" in its "oracular" and ultramontane interpretations.

28. This doctrine was taught authoritatively by the Fourth Lateran Council under Pope Innocent III, and in many other weighty pronouncements. It was jettisoned by Pope Pius XII in his Letter to the Archbishop of Boston of 8 August 1949, and again by the Second Vatican Council.

29. Migne, *PL*, 126, 221–249.

30. V. Soloviev, *La Russie et le l'Eglise Universelle*, p. xxi.

31. *Migne*, PL, 3, 1217ff.

32. Brian Tierney, *Foundations of the Conciliar Theory: the Contribution of the Medieval Canonists from Gratian to the Great Schism*: Cambridge, 1955: p. 53.

33. In the symposium *Le Concile et les Conciles*: Editions de Chevetogne, 1961.

34. Roman Catholics do not acknowledge the Council of Pisa as ecumenical, on the grounds that it was not convoked by the Pope; but how could it have been, since no one knew for certain who the Pope was? Presumably this council was as ecumenical as any other that has been summoned since the division between East and

West. In view of the complex problems concerning the papal succession that this would pose, it is certainly more convenient to deny it ecumenical status, on whatever pretext.

35. Mansi, xxvii, 590.
36. *De Gestis Concilii Basiliensis Commentariorum Libri II*: edited, and with English translation, by Denis Hay and W. K. Smith: Oxford Medieval Texts, Clarendon Press, 1967.
37. J. Gill, *Personalities of the Council of Florence*: Oxford, Blackwell, 1964.
38. ". . . . voces 'infallibilis' et 'infallibilitas' mutentur in 'ab errore immunis' et 'immunitas ab errore'." (*CL* t. 7, 444)
39. Latin text in Mansi, vol. lii, 1332–5.
40. David Mathew, *Lord Acton and his Times*: London, Eyre and Spottiswoode, 1968: p. 118.
41. Latin text in *CL*, t. 7, 944–952.
42. *The True and False Infallibility of the Popes* by Dr Joseph Fessler, late Bishop of St Polten and Secretary-General of the Vatican Council. Translated by Ambrose St John M.A.: London, Burns and Oates, 1875.
43. In the symposium *Infallibility in the Church: an Anglican-Catholic Dialogue*: London, Darton, Longman, and Todd, 1968.
44. Migne, PL xcvi, 1217.
45. V. de Waal, " 'De Ecclesia': an Anglican Comment", in *One in Christ: a Catholic Ecumenical Review*, vol. ii, no. 1, 1966.

3　THE POPE AND BIRTH CONTROL

1. cf. John Moorman, *A History of the Franciscan Order from its Origins to the year 1517*: Oxford, 1968: p. 408.
2. Article on "Conflicts with Rome" in *The Home and Foreign Review* (1864), quoted by Douglas Woodruff in his introduction to Acton, *Essays on Church and State*: London, Hollis and Carter, 1952.
3. *Enchiridion Symbolorum*: a collection of papal and conciliar documents edited originally by Henry Denzinger, and since brought up to date by various editors, the latest of whom is Father Adolf Schoenmetzer S.J. The current edition, 1965, runs to nearly a thousand pages. To find in them any reference to contraception earlier than 1930 is a matter of great difficulty. One of the most important documents, Sixtus V's bull *Effraenatam* is neither included nor referred to.
4. Published in England by the Oxford University Press. In 1967 a paperback edition (667 pp.) was published by the New American Library in their Mentor-Omega series, and is available in this country.

5. Noonan, *Contraception*, Mentor-Omega edition, pp. 447.
6. Cf. 'Humanae Vitae: an examination" by Hubert Campbell in *The Newman*, the journal of the Newman Association Trust, vol. 3, no. 4, October 1968. Dr Campbell is senior lecturer in medical statistics in the Welsh National School of Medicine and an adviser to the World Health Organisation.
7. This means that if an action has two results, one good and the other bad, the action may nevertheless be performed if the bad result is not directly intended; e.g., the bombing of a military objective which will involve also the destruction of non-combatants.
8. This expression seems to some extent to justify those who regard "Humanae Vitae" as a serious statement of the Pope's *opinion* rather than an authentic expression of the Church's magisterium, or teaching authority.
9. The Pope here ignores the witness of the married clergy of the Catholic Eastern rites, and also that of the clergy of the Orthodox churches. Everything is seen from an exclusively Latin and Roman point of view.

4 THE MINISTRY

1. Batiffol, *Primitive Catholicism*, p. 54.
2. Charisms; particular graces or gifts of the Holy Spirit given to individual Christians to help them in their work of advancing the spiritual wellbeing of others.
3. Dix, "The Ministry in the Church", in *The Apostolic Ministry*, edited by K. E. Kirk: London, Hodder and Stoughton, 1964; p. 190.
4. "If anyone says that in the Catholic Church there is not a hierarchy by divine ordination instituted, consisting of bishops, priests, and deacons: let him be anathema."
5. K. D. Mackenzie, sometime bishop of Brechin, on "Non-Episcopal Communions", in Kirk, *The Apostolic Ministry*.
6. Whitgift, Works, Parker Society 1851–3, vol. i, p. 6.
7. Norman Sykes, *Old Priest and New Presbyter*, Cambridge, 1956: p. 23.
8. T. M. Parker, "Feudal Episcopacy", in Kirk, *The Apostolic Ministry*, p. 386.
9. Translation in Bettenson, *Documents of the Christian Church*, p. 195.
10. Cf. Hans Küng, *The Church*, p. 336.
11. Erasmus, Letter to Albert of Brandenburg, of 19 October 1519.

12. Gregory Dix, *The Shape of the Liturgy*: London, Dacre Press, second edition, 1945, p. 245.
13. Dix, *The Shape of the Liturgy*, p. 746.
14. Cranmer, *Works*, Parker Society edition: vol. 1, pp. 28–30.
15. *The New Papal Credo and Orthodox-Catholic Relations* by Archbishop Athenagoras II of Thyateira and Great Britain: Greek and English text, 1969. Obtainable from The Fellowship of SS. Alban and Sergius, 52 Ladbroke Grove, London W.11.
16. Denzinger 2495.
17. Figures taken from *Herder Correspondence* for March 1969.
18. Free eucharists, on this pattern, are now familiar in many places on the Continent. They are not as yet authorised by the Roman Catholic bishops of England and Wales.

5 MONASTICISM

1. "Religious": a convenient technical term which designates any man or woman dedicated to God's service in community life under the three vows, whether monk, nun, friar, or clerk regular.
2. Cambridge, 1923.
3. P. 151 of the 1876 edition edited by Abbot Norbert Sweeney.
4. The White monks (Cistercians) remained faithful to their pursuit of husbandry, as they do to this day.
5. Reprinted in David Knowles, *The Historian and Character*: Cambridge, 1963.
6. Cf. Knowles, *The Religious Orders in England*, vol. iv, p. 462.
7. The reference is to the biblical translations of the late Ronald Knox.
8. Cf., *passim*, John Moorman, *A History of the Franciscan Order from its Origins to the Year 1517*: Oxford, The Clarendon Press, 1968.

6 EAST AND WEST

1. Cf. V. Lossky, *The Mystical Theology of the Eastern Church*: London, James Clarke, 1957, p. 179.
2. Robert of Bridlington, *The Bridlington Dialogue: an Exposition of the Rule of St. Augustine for the Life of the Clergy* translated by a Religious of C.S.M.V.: London, Mowbray, 1960.
3. In *Journal of Theological Studies*, October 1968.
4. This theory has been criticised by a Catholic theologian in a number of *JTS*, but its general approach seems more easily

harmonisable with reason and revelation than are other theories of the Fall.

5. An Orthodox critic of the encyclical "Humanae Vitae" has pointed out that in the Western theology of marriage it is the laws and processes of man's corrupted and fallen nature that are said to express the will of God. "Man's fallen life, and the natural processes to which he is subject in the fallen world constitute the norm on which the moral law of the Church is to be based. Man's natural life is regarded as that which he lives within the world as it is, as it is perceived by the senses, that in which he has fallen away from his original glory. There is no longer any recognition that this life is profoundly abnormal and unnatural where man is concerned . . . And there is consequently no recognition that the norm for what is natural for man, and hence for what constitutes the moral law, may lie in a completely different order of reality, and that to derive it from this world as it is, is to mistake human error and its consequences for divine ordinance." (Philip Sherard, "Humanae Vitae: Notes on the Encyclical Letter of Pope Paul VI", in *Sobornost* Winter-Spring 1969.)

6. John Gray, *Park: a Fantastic Story*: 2nd edition, Aylesford, St Albert's Press, 1966: p. 104.

7. Baptism by total immersion, still provided for by the Catholic and Anglican churches, though rarely practised, symbolises Christ's burial and resurrection, and our own death to sin and resurrection to eternal life.

8. Migne, *PG*, xlv, 88.

9. For indulgences see the bull "Unigenitus" of Pope Clement VI, the Instructions of Albert archbishop of Mainz, and Luther's Ninety-Five Theses: all printed in translation in Bettenson, *Documents of the Christian Church*, pp. 182–191.

10. Justification: the act by which God makes sinful man just; the change in a man's state when he passes from the state of sin to that of righteousness.

11. Imputation: the ascription to a person, by deliberate substitution, of the righteousness or guilt of another.

12. Lossky, *The Mystical Theology of the Eastern Church*, pp. 179–180.

13. John iv, 13–14.

14. Cf., for example, Panagiotis N. Trembelas, *Dogmatique de L'Eglise Orthodoxe Catholique*: Paris, Desclée, 1966, t. 1, pp. 324–348.

15. Article "A Propos de deux articles de l'abbé Laurentin" in *Présence Orthodoxe*: Paris, 1967, 4me trimestre, no. 1.

16. Book of Common Prayer, "Form for the Solemnization of Matrimony".

17. Reported in *The Tablet*, 5 October 1968.

7 *ECCLESIA SEMPER REFORMANDA*

1. The late Francis Spellman, Archbishop of New York.
2. The Bishop of Nottingham.
3. "Rescue the Pope", report of an address given by Fr Bernard Häring at Holy Cross Abbey, Colorado: *The Tablet*, 31 August 1968.
4. Francis Simons, Bishop of Indore, *Infallibility and the Evidence*: Springfield, Illinois, Templegate Publishers, 1968.
5. B. C. Butler, "The Church's One Foundation", in *The Tablet*, 14 December 1968.
6. "Nor was Peter superior to the church because of his primacy, for he is appointed by the church and for the church. . . . Wherefore Peter's primacy was within the church and not over it."
7. Cf. *Nicholas of Cusa* by Henry Brett: London, Methuen, 1932.
8. The Eastern churches cannot be held to have been adequately represented by the handful of Catholic Orientals (or "Uniates") who were present at Trent and Vatican I and II. Some of these have in any case suffered considerable latinisation both in their general outlook and liturgical practice. Nevertheless, the Catholic Eastern Churches are deserving of the greatest respect. Their faithfullness to the tradition of the Roman primacy in its essence, for which they have suffered much, and their special mission of interpreting the East to the West, gives them a vital rôle in any *rapprochement* between Catholicism and Orthodoxy.
9. Preface of the Mass for the Feast of the Kingship of Christ (the first Sunday in October).
10. Cf. *Hadrian the Seventh* by Frederick William Rolfe, Baron Corvo: London, Chatto and Windus, 1904; new edition in Penguin Books, 1968.

APPENDIX A: THE WIDER ECUMENISM

1. Rodney Collin Smith (1909–1956), who wrote under the name of Rodney Collin, was a follower of Ouspensky who became a Catholic in 1954, when he was living and working in South America. "By temperament, inclination, study, and by the country in which I have to work", he says, "I became a Roman Catholic. I had already anticipated this several years ago. It only needed the right moment and opportunity. For this time is a crossroads. Other people, at the same crossroads, might join different religions,

though it seems to me that Roman Catholicism has the greatest reserve of esoteric truth."

This quotation is from the extracts from his letters published under the title *The Theory of Conscious Harmony*. His principal works are *The Theory of Celestial Influence* and *The Theory of Eternal Life*. There is also a small selection from his notebooks called *The Mirror of Light*.

2. Those who are unfamiliar with the idea of a traditional society may be referred to the writings of Ananda Coomeraswamy, Frithjof Schuon, René Guenon, and Marco Pallis, among others; and also to Miss Kathleen Raine's recent book of essays *Defending Ancient Springs*, and the quarterly magazine *Studies in Comparative Religion*.

3. It scarcely needs to be said that a traditional society is not one in which human inventiveness is stifled and which involves a return to a state of "primitivism". It is a question of the *direction* which is set for the human intelligence, which would not be that which spends millions of pounds in torturing a monkey and sending it in a spacecraft round the moon while the earth's resources are being more and more polluted and destroyed and millions of the earth's inhabitants are starving.

APPENDIX B: THE NEW ENGLISH LITURGY

1. Father Bernard Häring, at a public meeting in Glasgow on 4 July 1969. Report in *The Tablet* for 12.7.1969.
2. Since this paragraph was written the abolition of the *Missale Romanum*, together with the variant missals of the Dominican, Carmelite, and other rites, has been decreed. Appeals for the retention of the ancient use as a permissible alternative to the so-called "Missa Normativa" have gone not only unheard but unacknowledged.

INDEX